THE
FRANCHISE
ADVANTAGE

THE FRANCHISE ADVANTAGE

Make it work for you

by Donald D. Boroian
and Patrick J. Boroian

National BestSeller Corporation

Library of Congress number: 87-62022

ISBN: 0-931073-03-0

National BestSeller Corporation
955 American Lane
Schaumburg, IL 60173
312/240-7720

National BestSeller Staff

President: Mike Michaelson
Project Editor: Michael Sweeney
Editorial and Research Assistance: David Eickemeyer
  Arline Fisher
  Glynis A. Steadman

Printed in the United States of America

To the American entrepreneur.

Acknowledgements

The authors would like to acknowledge several special contributors without whom the writing of this book would not have been possible. Each of these people have both enriched our lives with their friendship and have contributed greatly to our knowledge of franchising: Arthur Lipper, Publisher, *Venture* magazine; David Epstein, Investment Banker, J.H. Chapman Group; Jules W. Lederer, former Chairman, Budget Rent A Car; Andrew Kostecka, Franchise Specialist with the U.S. Department of Commerce; Edward Byron Smith, Jr., the Northern Trust Company; and Kegham and Charles Giragosian, formerly Presidents and Chairmen of Chicken Unlimited.

In addition, we would like to thank Mike Michaelson, President, and Michael Sweeney, Editor, of National BestSeller Corporation for their assistance in preparing this book. And our gratitude, as well, to Richard Gosswiller, Francorp's Vice President of Marketing who coordinated the project. Finally, our thanks to these other members of the Francorp staff for their helpful suggestions: Michael P. Boroian, Executive Vice President; Annette Knight, Vice President, Western Region; James L. Thompson, Vice President, Finance; James R. Beznik, Vice President and General Counsel; Patricia A. Clark, Director of Human Resources; Michael H. Baum, Creative Director; David Chandler, Director of Strategic Planning and Research; Mark C. Siebert, Director of International Relations; Gary Kisel, Joseph Busch, and Ken R. Friedman, Senior Consultants; Linda F. Brakel, Director of Operations Consulting; Loretta Pyrdek, Assistant Director of International Relations; and Lauren A. Maxwell, Franchise Research Coordinator.

Contents

FOREWORD:

By Arthur Lipper III,
Chairman and Editor-in-Chief,
Venture magazine

If owning one's own business is the American dream, then franchising is the best manner of achieving many of the benefits of business ownership for most people.

I think of franchising as the using of a toll expressway rather than chancing less direct, frequently winding, and, to the traveler unfamiliar with the territory, confusing roads. Expressways are well-marked, have service stations in predictable locations, and have toll collectors from whom advice and directions may be gained. Those attempting to travel between the same points as connected by an expressway, but using lesser roads, may not get there at all, or are subject to a much broader range of estimated arrival times. If predictability of result is important to the traveler, it is usually better to use an expressway.

The best thing about franchising as a product and/or service distribution mechanism is that it is one of those synergistic business relationships in which all of the parties have to benefit for any of them to achieve long-term success. In most cases, for the franchisee to succeed the franchisor has to do a good job of providing service. Equally, for the franchisor to succeed the franchisee must profit. There is no such thing as a successful franchisor who does not have successful franchisees. Conversely, successful franchisees usually are a result of a franchisor's successful product creation, franchise development, marketing and franchisee selection, training, and servicing.

Don Boroian is one of those uniquely gifted individuals who has demonstrated both a determination to succeed and a sensitivity to the needs of others. As both a successful husband and parent, Don has manifested an intelligent application of love and leadership. In much the same manner, and using some of the same management techniques, Don, with his sons Patrick and Michael, has built the largest and most successful franchise consulting firm in the world. Much as *Venture* magazine has as its primary mission "profit education," Francorp, Inc. is in the business of guiding those who seek to guide others in the creation and pursuit of profit.

In our free-market economic system, a commercial entity can only succeed over a period of time if it is successful in creating and delivering value to its customers. Franchising is a system—perhaps the best system—for delivering value to consumers. Francorp offers a range of consulting services to those who have already proven they have created a product for which there is a demand and which can be produced and delivered at a profit. Francorp's function in the area of franchise packaging can be simply described as the creation and broadening of a market by "duplicating success." If I were ever in the position of owning a non-personality dependent, multi-location, consumer product business I'd probably grow it through franchising and certainly use Francorp on a continuing consulting basis.

The Franchise Advantage represents a distillation of Don and Pat Boroian's years in the success-duplication business. Employing theory, common sense, case histories, and anecdotes from extensive personal experience, the Boroians shed light on the complex series of decisions which go into the creation of a franchised business. This isn't "franchising made simple." Franchising isn't a simple field, and Don and Pat don't try to make the answers appear cut and dried. Rather, they go to the heart of each issue frankly and honestly, asking all the right questions and revealing answers that work.

Franchising is "the future" of product and service distribution, and those who understand the process will be in a better position to benefit therefrom. *The Franchise Advantage* will help those considering franchising from the perspective of the franchisee *or* the franchisor. Personally, if I were entering into franchising in either role, I can't think of anyone whose advice I'd want more than that of Don and Pat Boroian.

INTRODUCTION:
An American Business Phenomenon

The cafeteria on 45th Street in New York City had been doing business for about 60 years. Founded by one of the city's fast-food pioneers, it had seen some good times and some bad. Lately, they had been mostly bad, with losses of $75,000 on a volume of $600,000 in a single year. Then came the conversion of the slumping cafeteria to a Burger King outlet and it wasn't long before the unit was serving 5,000 customers a day and netting the franchisee $260,000 on $1.5 million sales. At the time of the switch, one of the former owners noted, somewhat wryly, that if he were to walk down to the store, take down the Burger King sign, and put up another that read "Fred's Burgers," volume would plunge by 60 percent by the end of the day.

Such is the power of franchising. But in any successful franchise the name is only one important factor. Even more critical to success are the franchise's structure, organization, system, training, and level of support. To understand the success of franchising, you must first understand what franchising is: a unique business growth strategy governed by a unique set of rules.

Approach a neophyte franchisor—perhaps one who has proudly attended the grand opening of his first franchise unit—and ask what kind of business he is in. He'll likely reply that he derives his livelihood from the pizza business, the auto tune-up business, the instant-print business, or whatever else describes the product or service his units are merchandising. Put that same question to the same franchisor a year down the road when grand openings are old hat and the term "a franchise chain" has become a reality, and he'll probably answer you correctly this time: "the franchise business."

Should you decide to follow the steps that we'll outline in the following chapters, you will find yourself learning a whole new kind of business. Jules Lederer, founder of Budget Rent A Car, learned that important lesson through trial and error: "I've found that even astute businesspeople don't always understand franchising. It is a very different form of distribution and expansion than many people are used to." John Amico, a client and friend, echoes this thought. John, who has parlayed his Hair Performers salons into a chain of more than 300 franchises, notes: "You might be terrific in the hair business, but that doesn't mean that you will have a successful franchise. I learned that franchising is a business in and of itself, and requires specific expertise." (You'll find more hints from these and other successful franchisors in Chapters 5 and 6.)

The franchising expertise you will need will touch every aspect of your business. A start-up franchisor needs the help of attorneys, accountants, strategic planners, and specialists in sales, operations, and marketing—in fact, the broad range of business disciplines that one might expect to call upon when launching and marketing a new concept. But with a major difference. It is vital that the attorney you select offer the very specialized knowledge needed to guide you through a bewildering maze of franchise law. Similarly, the accountant, systems people, and all of the other professionals you hire should possess this intimate familiarity with the highly distinctive and decidedly complex business of franchising. It is because of the acutely specialized nature of franchising and the importance of coordinating these services under one roof that we formed a consulting firm in 1976 to meet this need. And it is, of course, the reason for this book.

Entering blindly into franchising, as our friend and colleague Jules Lederer succinctly notes, is like trying to fly an airplane without instruction. But if you make the right moves, franchising can jet you to your goal faster than any other growth system.

What is franchising?

There is more than one kind of franchising, but for the purposes of this book we will almost always be discussing "business-format" franchising. Business-format franchising is a method of business expansion whereby a business owner or manager allows someone to market products or services under his name and trademark and in strict adherence to a system he prescribes. In return, the franchisee, as that person (or organization) is called, pays a fee and, usually, an ongoing royalty. Moreover, the franchisee pays all of the costs of getting into his or her own business.

As you can see, if you are seeking a growth opportunity for your present business, franchising unquestionably presents an attractive, enticing option. But before you succumb to its wiles, consider that a franchisor/franchisee relationship is not like a friendship, a courtship, or even an engagement. It is more like a marriage—the forging of a contract under which two partners with mutual interests agree to work in harmony toward a common objective. And, like a marriage, it is not something that should be entered into lightly. Because if the partners are not compatible, the ensuing divorce can be traumatic and costly.

So, if you are a confirmed bachelor, unable or unwilling to give up your total business freedom, franchising might not be for you. On the other hand, when both partners work together, the franchise method of doing business can produce a win-win-win scenario for all concerned. For the franchisor, it is a means of expansion that does not require huge infusions of capital. It also can provide an effective mechanism for achieving deep market penetration and saturation before the competition is able to make a move. Franchising is a viable alternative to the costly and time-consuming practice of opening additional company stores. With franchisees to help raise capital, share risks, and provide dedicated, vested management, corporate growth and expansion can be swift and relatively painless.

For the franchisee it is a shot at attaining the American dream of owning a business—but with much of the risk removed. In effect, the franchisee is able to launch a new business without any of the usual attendant growing pains. Someone else has already made—and corrected—the most important mistakes, ironed out most of the wrinkles, and invented a system that works. It is like a cook using a recipe created and tested by a master chef; he or she can be pretty confident of getting good results at the first attempt. And there is that additional comfort level that franchisees derive from the availability of ongoing support services— the knowledge that while they are in business for themselves, they never are in business by themselves. It also means being able to draw from collective strength in buying and advertising.

From the consumers' standpoint, a franchise offers the assurance of consistency. Consumers have come to expect that the pizza they buy in San Francisco will be identical to one they received from the same franchise in Boston. Ditto for haircuts, hamburgers, and hotel rooms.

Who should read this book?

Of course, franchising is not the answer for every company, as we will show later on. However, it does have a broad-based appeal that cuts across a remarkably diverse variety of products and services. For example, the U.S. Department of Commerce *Franchise Opportunities Handbook* lists 45 distinct categories of businesses (for a detailed listing, see Chapter 4). Within each of those categories are dozens of different types of businesses that run the gamut from auto muffler shops to yogurt stands, with companies ranging from A & W Restaurants, Inc. to Ziebart Rustproofing Company. Certainly, a method of distribution that now accounts for one-third of all retail sales and which the U.S. Department of Commerce hails as "the wave of the future" deserves the consideration of prudent businesspeople for myriad reasons. We believe that the information we have assembled in this volume can be helpful—and, in some cases, critical—to the decision by business owners and managers as to whether or not franchising is the right expansion system for them. In particular, we'll be talking to the following people:

Successful entrepreneurs

Franchising is a dynamic force that the entrepreneur simply cannot afford to overlook. Consider that in the 10 years between 1977 and 1987 the number of companies offering business-format franchises doubled to more than 2,000. In the same period, the number of individual franchise units in operation grew to nearly 500,000.

A successful entrepreneur is the individual with the dream who also has the tenacity and the smarts to turn that dream into a business reality. Of course, a great idea is not enough to launch a successful franchise program. The graveyard of "great business ideas" that failed is very large, indeed. By the same token, many businesses offering mediocre products or services have been extremely successful. Often, the difference between success and failure is the existence of a solid system to support the entrepreneur's bright idea. And for a business to grow and expand swiftly through franchising, that idea and its supporting system must be teachable and replicable.

Executives of companies at the crossroads

This seems to be the age of corporate titans doing battle in the business arena with dramatic takeovers, buyouts, mergers, and corporate restructurings. From the sidelines the smaller company, perhaps the company at the crossroads of growth, can learn an important lesson. The big boys get bigger by applying a concept that we like to call "channel power." Simply stated, if you have a channel of distribution, you have power.

Within the franchise industry, there are some classic examples of the expert wielding of channel power. Ask yourself why Transamerica Corporation, an insurance company, would acquire Budget Rent A Car. Or why PepsiCo would want to buy Kentucky Fried Chicken for $841 million? One answer to both questions is channel power. Most Americans, when renting a car, spend about $9 on insurance—even though they may be adequately covered under their own auto insurance policies. A car-rental company provides, quite literally, a captive market for an insurance company that—over the course of a year—can add up to a staggeringly large book of brand-new business.

Or take PepsiCo, Inc., which owns Taco Bell and Pizza Hut. At the time it acquired Kentucky Fried Chicken, about 70 percent of those fast-food outlets were selling Coca-Cola. With this buyout PepsiCo obtained the potential for converting many of these units to its own soft-drink brands. The result was that PepsiCo took away one percent of Coca-Cola's domestic sales.

Franchising can bring this kind of channel power even to small businesses. If your business has two or three units, and you're wondering how to expand to 100 or 1,000, franchising can provide the capital you need to get there before someone else does. Consider that Wendy's International grew to more than 3,800 outlets in only 18 years. And then look at similar businesses that have expanded the conventional way by opening company stores. In the case of the latter, you'll find that in twice the time most haven't achieved half the growth. The reason is that franchising provides a fast route to market penetration, market saturation, and proliferation.

Corporate decision makers

It is all too easy when discussing franchising to focus on fast-food chains, but the fact remains that of the estimated $591

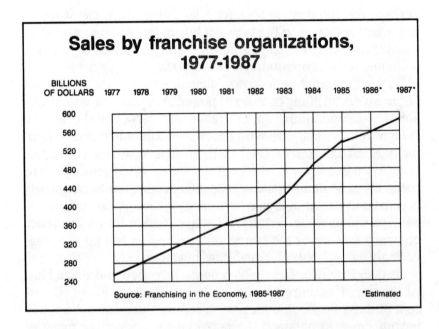

Sales by franchise organizations, 1977-1987

BILLIONS OF DOLLARS — 1977 1978 1979 1980 1981 1982 1983 1984 1985 1986* 1987*

Source: Franchising in the Economy, 1985-1987   *Estimated

billion in sales rung up in 1987 by franchised businesses, only about 10 percent was generated by restaurants. Even in business-format franchising, restaurants account for only about one-third of all sales. By the same token, it is a mistake to assume that franchising is an expansion method used exclusively by small entrepreneurs. Franchising is not only an extraordinary tool for helping make small companies big, it also can be a catalyst in assisting big companies to become bigger. Atlantic Richfield, for example, used franchising to create a chain of more than 700 am/pm mini markets. Of course, a large company tends to seek its level in the marketplace and then looks for fractional points of growth. And while growth gains at this level may not appear to be as spectacular, they can have dynamic impact on the bottom line. Large companies encumbered with such constraints as tightly-budgeted investment and reinvestment capital, simply lack the flexibility to react quickly in the way that a small company or a fly-by-the-seat-of-the-pants entrepreneur can. Handling the controls of a large corporation is more like flying a 747—you can't make sharp turns.

But the goals can be the same. Franchising allows the large company to expand rapidly with a minimal drain on its capital resources and without the need to deploy large numbers of personnel. It's a fast ticket to market saturation, enabling the corporation to penetrate new market segments while cutting overhead and administrative costs and decentralizing management down to the unit level.

Franchising also provides a creative means of refinancing—raising fresh capital by selling off company-owned units as franchises. The transition can be especially smooth when an employee who manages a unit buys a franchise. Presto, a highly trained and now totally committed business owner is in charge. Gone is corporate investment in facilities, equipment, and inventory; the burden of payroll; and the cost of an employee-benefit package. Yet franchising produces immediate cash flow and continuing income for the company.

Thus, we suggest this book as a franchising primer for corporate decision makers, including chief executive officers, vice presidents of marketing, and other division-level managers with bottom-line responsibilities.

The fact is that for anyone who owns or operates a successful business, the times have never been better to consider expansion via franchising. Record numbers of people are starting their own businesses, as evidenced by new incorporations, now numbering more than three-quarters of a million a year. At the same time, big corporations, including many *Fortune* 500 companies, are stripping away layers of middle management employees with layoffs and early retirements. In fact, in 1986 alone, more than 12 million white-collar jobs were eliminated in the U.S. This has created a pool of individuals looking to start up businesses—people with capital to invest from pension funds and profit sharing, and with equity in their homes and other bankable assets. Franchising offers the expansion-minded company an excellent opportunity to tap into this reservoir of management talent and capital.

Franchisors seeking improvements

Yes, we strongly recommend this book to franchisors seeking to improve existing franchise programs. If you have been intimately involved in running a franchise company, you may not realize just how much the industry is changing and how quickly these changes are occurring. Over the course of a year, in our offices and during field consulting assignments, we work with a broad spectrum of America's most successful franchisors. We constantly are surprised at how dated many of their programs are. We have met with franchisors—well-known, well-established companies—who were using obsolete legal documents that were drafted before much of today's intricate web of franchise law was passed. Other franchisors are simply failing to recognize the growing tendency of disenchanted franchisees to organize.

Franchising is not only the most efficient system for rapid expansion, it is also among the *fastest changing* business systems. We believe that many franchisors, successful though they are, could enjoy even greater levels of achievement if they were to make some fundamental adjustments or avoid such basic errors as selling territories too large or locating franchises too close together. It is our business to stay abreast of the state of the art and it is our intention to share with you in the pages that follow the most current information available about franchising.

Investors, investment bankers, and lenders

Franchising offers a wide-open opportunity for investors, lenders, and others with available capital. After all, franchising is a business system oriented to growth, and growth is what investment is all about. There are two major levels at which the financier might become a player: 1. By providing capital to the franchisor; 2. By capitalizing the franchisee. Franchising's capital needs vary, although those controlling the purse strings should keep in mind that the requirement is not for seed capital, but for second-stage expansion capital based on a successful prototype. There is a place in franchise financing for asset-based and collateral-based lenders, as well as for venture capitalists. Capital requirements may range from $50,000 for a restaurant equipment package to several millions of dollars for a series of new company-owned units to function as prototypes in the development of new territories.

Although a perceived negative of a typical franchise development program is an inherent lack of collateral or asset value, one offsetting advantage is the enticing statistic of franchisee staying power—the fact that, according to the U.S. Department of Commerce, franchisees have a failure rate of less than five percent per year, whereas various authorities estimate that between 65 and 90 percent of new businesses fail within the first five years. At least one major bank has recognized the advantage of franchising. The Royal Bank of Canada, through a special franchise loan department, has backed franchisors and franchisees to the tune of more than $400 million.

Prospective franchisees

Suppose you were planning to get married. Wouldn't you want to know as much as possible about your prospective spouse *before* you took your vows?

So it is with the person interested in buying a franchise. Although this book is written largely for the prospective franchisor, if you are a prospective franchisee your decision concerning which franchise to buy can be greatly enhanced by an intimate knowledge of the methods of operation and the underlying philosophy that guide those with whom you plan to enter into a business relationship.

For example, as a franchisee, you should become acquainted with at least the basics of franchise law, much of which was enacted for the protection of the franchisee. You should also have a thorough understanding of the franchise agreement itself, including how it is structured and why. Similarly, a franchisee will find it useful to know how a franchise program typically is planned and marketed, how franchise fees and royalty payments are established, how group buying and cooperative advertising work, and what generally to expect in terms of training and support.

In our consulting business, clients often ask us to help them select franchisees. As a result, we and the franchise sales specialists on our staff have the opportunity to interview a large number of prospective franchisees. We believe that the more knowledgeable they are about the franchise industry, the better their chances of success. In the "marriage" between franchisor and franchisee the greater the understanding and appreciation each has for the other, the more harmonious and successful that relationship will be.

The general reader

Franchising is one of the most significant economic developments of the twentieth century. But it is also the manifestation of a far larger social trend—one that on the surface seems self-contradictory. On the one hand, franchising does result in a certain amount of uniformity, much scorned by critics. But at a deeper level, franchising has been an anathema to regimentation. By allowing more people to successfully own businesses than ever before, franchising has given these individuals an alternative to climbing the corporate ladder and toeing the corporate line. At the same time, franchising has enabled entrepreneur-owners of relatively small businesses to effectively compete in the marketplace against large corporations. Franchising makes rapid growth possible without huge amounts of capital, which means that a well-run business with a point of difference has a better chance of expanding than ever before. At one time, small businesses could easily be shut out of a market by a company willing to "buy" that market. It can still happen, but when a business is able to attract new capital and motivated managers through franchising, the likelihood that a big guy will be able to throw his weight around diminishes.

Franchising also fascinates because it changes. It is constantly being applied in new ways by different kinds of organizations, large and small. Anyone seriously interested in studying the nature of capitalism would have to go far to find a more creative use of it than franchising.

What Ray Kroc Did That Was Different

1

Somewhere, someone's Uncle Matthew is smiling. Back in the late 1960s when he was a restaurant-equipment manufacturer's rep, Matthew traveled extensively around the country. On his travels, he started noticing more and more McDonald's restaurants popping up and he read in a food-service trade magazine that in little more than 10 years the chain had grown to close to 1,000 units. Responsible for this phenomenal growth was an innovative concept known as "franchising." Matthew liked to play the stock market. Figuring he knew a good thing when he saw it, he bought 100 shares of McDonald's at $22.50 apiece on the first day they were offered. Twenty years later, those shares are worth around $4,000 each—a return of a cool $400,000 (plus dividends) on an investment of $2,250.

That particular American fable is apocryphal. But it *could* have happened in just that way, because the meteoric rise of

McDonald's stock is exactly as stated. In fact, it was first offered in April, 1965 at an opening price of $22.50, and by the end of the first day it already had climbed to $30. By month's end it reached $50. The stock continued to perform and was hailed as one of the hottest stocks of the decade.

Since then, McDonald's has become synonymous with franchising throughout America and abroad. Not only is it the premier fast-food retailer with more than 10,000 units, it is also the largest holder of retail real estate in the world. McDonald's decision, early in its history, to own the land and buildings at its store sites, propelled the franchise into a strong financial position. By the late 1970s, McDonald's owned more than 50 percent (now more than 60 percent) of the sites of its outlets and was collecting rent amounting to 8.5 percent of unit sales over and above its standard royalty of 3 percent, while competitors were collecting royalties alone. As a result, the company now is able to generate most of its capital internally.

As for its popularity and universality, McDonald's claims that in a given year 96 percent of all Americans walks through its doors, while 59 percent of the population visits a McDonald's during the course of a month. It is a company that can boast of having given one out of every 15 Americans his or her first job and of dispensing five percent of all Coca-Cola sold worldwide. And not only does McDonald's control a large share of the hamburger and Coke markets, but, with the successful introduction of Chicken McNuggets in 1980, it has become the second largest retailer of chicken in the country.

Compare this growth and dominance in the marketplace to the growth pattern of another hamburger chain, White Castle, which was begun in the early 1900s and might have been able to corner the fast-food market had it franchised. Instead, the owner of White Castle decided that he wouldn't buy anything he couldn't pay for, so he embarked on a slow program of expansion, plowing the profits of existing stores into building additional units, one at a time. Today, after 70 years in the business, White Castle has approximately 300 units. That's one-thirtieth of the number McDonald's established in less than half the time.

The beginnings

Franchising, of course, did not begin with the construction of the first golden arch. What Ray Kroc and McDonald's did was to revolutionize a system that had existed for years. Franchising became prominent in the 19th century as railroad and utility companies looked for ways to speed their growth. By selling subsidiary rights to their names and/or systems, these entities could, in effect, more quickly open a new section of track or a new electric plant in the next town.

However, the Singer Sewing Machine Company is generally acknowledged as the first retail franchisor. In the 1850s, Singer established a network of salesmen/dealers who paid Singer for the right to distribute sewing machines in a particular region. Although these arrangements were not completely successful for Singer and were discontinued after about 10 years, Singer had sown the seeds for franchising's future use and eventual universal acceptance.

The automobile industry, the petroleum industry, and the soft-drink producers were all manufacturers that turned to franchising in the late 1800s and early 1900s because they lacked channels of distribution for their products. They could not afford to buy the property and build the buildings to house multiple stores or outlets, hire the managers and clerks to staff them, and, in the case of the soft-drink producers (because long-distance shipments were uneconomical), supply them with the inventory to sell. Instead, they sold the franchises to people who would take on the responsibility—financially and operationally—of creating dealerships, gas stations, and bottling companies. These product and trademark franchises (granting the exclusive right to sell a given product in a specified territory or at a specified location) were successful in spurring the growth of the franchise phenomenon, but their influence began to wane after World War II, as another system of franchising grew in popularity.

Business-format franchising—the early years

After World War II, retailing began a gradual shift from product-
to service-orientation. As the American middle class became
more mobile and began relocating in significant numbers to the
suburbs, restaurants or drive-ins specializing in quick take-out
or eat-in meals emerged. While most were local operations or
regionalized mini-chains, franchised outlets such as A & W and
Tastee Freez grew in popularity across the country. They were
joined in the 1950s by McDonald's, Burger King, Dunkin' Donuts, Kentucky Fried Chicken and other national food franchises,
but by then franchising was undergoing a subtle, but important,
evolution.

Instead of simply granting a license to distribute or sell a product, the growing food franchises—joined by non-food businesses
such as Holiday Inns, Midas mufflers, and H & R Block—were
employing a significantly different form of franchising. These
franchisors sold the right to adopt an entire business concept,
from signs and advertising to recipes and uniforms, and often
the licensees were people with no previous business experience.
Although some business-format franchisors (as they came to be
called) required franchisees to purchase certain supplies and
products from them, their major source of income was the sale
of their proven business system.

It was into this fast-changing business atmosphere that Ray Kroc
and McDonald's entered in the mid-1950s. Having observed bur-
geoning fast-food franchises during his days as a traveling salesman, Kroc had assessed what he perceived to be the strengths
and weaknesses of franchising, and used them as guides in building McDonald's. By using business-format franchising to successfully create a huge business out of franchised hamburger
restaurants, Kroc effectively altered the way people and companies thought about business expansion.

Kroc & McDonald's

While the public perception of Ray Kroc was that of hamburger king and franchisor *extraordinaire*, he was, above all else, a master salesman. Kroc did not invent McDonald's, fast-food, or franchising, but he refined them to a degree that no one else has done, before or since. Then he sold the concept—one hamburger stand at a time—to both his franchisees and the American public. The approach Kroc applied to franchising was as obvious and revolutionary as the one Henry Ford had applied to the mass-production of automobiles. And the results the two men and their companies realized—fabulous success and a lasting impact on America's socio-economic structure—were identical.

Kroc's sales background included a long stint peddling paper cups and a disastrous stab at selling real estate during the 1920s' Florida land boom. In the 1930s, he obtained the rights to a multiple-spindle mixer called the Multimixer, and began selling that—mainly to the restaurants and lunch counters that had previously been paper-cup customers. His cross-country sales jaunts brought him into contact with a multitude of food service independents, chains, and even fledgling franchises, such as Tastee Freez and Dairy Queen. Although he was not a food-service professional, Kroc was an interested observer in the business, and was always—both in his paper-cup and Multimixer days—suggesting new uses for his products to his customers.

By the early 1950s, Multimixer sales had dropped so low that they were a threat to the existence of Kroc's company. Then came a revelation. In the normal course of events, most of Kroc's customers used only one Multimixer, with large lunch counters and ice cream shops perhaps having two. Yet a hamburger stand in San Bernardino, California—run by Dick and Mac McDonald—had recently purchased its tenth Multimixer and was using at least three or four at any given time. At a loss to understand how a hamburger stand could need so many Multimixers—and hoping to pick up a few pointers to boost his sales—Kroc visited the brothers' stand in 1954. He was astounded by the sight of masses of people standing in line to buy 15-cent hamburgers at the sales windows of a little octagonal building. He was also struck by the speed, efficiency, and cleanliness of the operation. After meeting the McDonald brothers, Kroc knew he must somehow get involved with the phenomenal success of their restaurant.

Kroc learned that the brothers were interested in franchising their so-called Speedy Service System. In fact, they had already sold the rights to copy their name, menu, building, and general system to a handful of franchisees, and were looking at the possibility of further expansion. Envisioning selling at least a pair of Multimixers to every new McDonald's, Kroc convinced the brothers to give him a chance as their new franchising agent, and began his relationship with McDonald's, which would continue until the day he died in 1984.

While Kroc was certain that the brothers' concept of selling hamburgers was sound, he concluded that the hands-off method they were using for franchising was flawed. The brothers' first new franchisees were left more or less on their own after being provided with plans for the building and the Speedy Service System, and some were drastically changing the initial concept to suit their own ideas or tastes. Franchisees were even adding roast beef, hot dogs, tacos, and other items to the supposedly sacrosanct—and proven—10-item menu the brothers had perfected.

Kroc had come to realize—from his days as a salesman, calling on various food-service franchises—that the approach to franchising the brothers had taken was pretty much the approach the rest of the food-service franchising industry was using. Franchisors would pitch the concept to potential franchisees, then issue rights and provide plans and manuals to anyone who could pay the franchise fee. Some would even offer a week or two of training to their new franchisees. However, this was often the last contact the franchisee had with the franchisors, who would move on to the next sales opportunity. Usually, these franchisors were more concerned with selling new franchises than providing support or advice to existing franchisees. In Kroc's view, these franchisors were taking a short-sighted approach to the expansion

of their businesses. He thought they were committing slow sui-
cide by not tending to the roots of their future success—the
franchisees.

When Kroc took over the franchising of McDonald's, he was
determined not to make the mistakes he had witnessed in other
franchises. It was his firm belief that a franchisor's success depended on the success of its individual franchises. His idea was
to provide the franchisees with support, training, and the general
business know-how to succeed. And, he correctly surmised that
as each franchisee prospered the entire chain would grow stronger.
Making his franchisees happy and successful was no different
to Kroc than what he had done when he was a paper-cup and
Multimixer salesman. To him, both endeavors involved creating
success by finding a way to make his product—be it cups or hamburger stands—profitable for his customers, or, in the case of
McDonald's, his franchisees. By basing the franchising of
McDonald's on this simple and obvious approach, Ray Kroc transformed the eating habits of America, and built McDonald's into
the king of fast food and a giant in the world of franchising.

Franchising's boom years

Perhaps the most significant sign of franchising's arrival as an
accepted and desirable business practice occurred on April 15,
1965, when stock in McDonald's was first offered for sale. As
we have noted, the value of the stock more than doubled in less
than a month, and continued steadily upward. (After 20 years,
the value of a single share had grown to approximately 175 times
the initial offering price.) Soon afterwards, Holiday Inns, Kentucky Fried Chicken, and other franchises began selling stock.
By the late 1960s, national chains such as McDonald's, Burger
Chef, Holiday Inns, and Kentucky Fried Chicken were nearing
or had passed the 1,000-unit mark. As the 1970s dawned,
franchising—led most visibly by fast-food chains—had become
deeply assimilated into the American way of life and business.
New franchises were springing up—and, quite often, dying off—

practically overnight. Successes in the field included new categories of franchises—such as business and health services—or new businesses within proven categories. New entries in the fast-food arena, for example, included pizza, Mexican, and other ethnic restaurants.

But everything was not completely rosy during the aggressive expansions of the late 1960s and early 1970s. For one thing, the advantages of franchising couldn't overcome major management errors. Burger Chef, for example, was rapidly catching up to McDonald's in number of units when it was acquired by General Foods in 1968. General Foods not only halted the expansion program, but began *losing* franchisees soon afterwards. By the time General Foods unloaded the then-money-losing chain in the mid-1970s, there were less than 300 outlets, down from a high of 1,200. Other highly publicized failures of this period included Minnie Pearl Fried Chicken restaurants (due to lack of a solid operational format and the greed of the promoter) and Arthur Murray Dance Studios, another franchise that traded heavily on a famous name and provided minimal support to franchisees.

Franchises that successfully rode the boom and continued to prosper and proliferate into the 1980s were a disparate mix, ranging from quick lube centers to employment agencies. Automotive service franchises, including AAMCO Transmission and Midas mufflers, became more important and popular as the price of cars rose and people began keeping older cars longer, and, consequently, started caring for them more extensively. Today, muffler, transmission, brake, lube, rustproofing, car rental, and other automotive franchises are common sights. Ethnic foods—led by pizza and Mexican food—made serious inroads in the fast-food world in the late 1970s, and are among the most popular outlets today. Pizza restaurants—first Shakey's, then current leader Pizza Hut and close competitor Domino's—successfully challenged the dominance of regional and neighborhood pizza places. Mexican restaurants—such as Taco Bell—established their popularity after educating consumers who were not familiar with the cuisine. Business service franchises—varying from instant printers to temporary personnel agencies to computer dealers and servicers—are popular in large cities and suburbs, and have begun to spread strongly outside of major metropolitan areas.

Conversion franchises

The late 1970s saw major growth in a third type of franchising after product distribution and business-format franchising: conversion franchising. Conversion franchises are exactly what their name implies—franchisees converted from independents or small chains in the franchisor's line of business. While there are examples of small-scale conversions in fast-food, hotels and motels, and other widely franchised businesses, the most successful efforts in this category came about in the 1970s and early 1980s in two businesses that had previously experienced little franchising: real estate and home remodeling/repairs.

In the 1960s, Anthony Yniguez and his Southern California-based Red Carpet Realty experienced the first large-scale success in converting independent real estate offices to franchisees sharing a unified name. By offering the strength of advertising in a large region—and, eventually, nationally—along with training programs and a referral network, Red Carpet appealed to the sensibilities and the bottom line of independents who saw that working together under one banner was more effective than competing with each other. Art Bartlett intensely studied Yniguez' approach and system, then "borrowed" it (as he fully admits) when he founded Century 21. Starting in 1971 with one office, the Century 21 chain grew spectacularly through conversion franchising to more than 7,500 offices by 1979. (Century 21 was acquired in an exchange of stock with Trans World Corp. in 1979, and was sold to Metropolitan Life for more than $250 million in 1985.)

Conversion franchising has also been successfully applied to the home remodeling/repair business, an industry that has long been a bastion of local, independent operators. Two of the leaders in this young segment of franchising are Mr. Build, begun in 1981 by Art Bartlett (after he grew tired of his post-Century 21 retirement), and Dial One International, founded by a group of former Century 21 executives. (After five years, Mr. Build has 550 franchises; Dial One has 700.)

Both franchisors have enlisted formerly independent building and remodeling contractors in a wide range of trades from painting to plumbing. The franchisor provides management training for its convert, plugs it into an extensive referral network, and, with each new convert, builds the collective advertising power of the entire system. Conversion franchising works best in a fragmented industry where no one organization has a strong national identity. It gives franchisees greater marketing muscle, buying power, and, to some degree, improved business systems. The major drawback to conversion franchising—in any field—is the reluctance that many independent businesspeople feel when asked to subvert their name and identity to that of a large franchised chain, especially if they do not perceive a clear and present need or market advantage.

Innovations

Maintaining an edge is very important in franchising, as it is in any competitive business. By offering something new or an improvement on something tried-and-true, franchises can build or increase their market shares. Three of the best examples of franchising innovations are easily illustrated:

1. **New Products.** When Century 21 was acquired in the mid-1980s by Metropolitan Life, it became able to offer insurance directly to its customers. Today, it is estimated that 70 percent of the people who purchase homes from Century 21 buy their homeowners insurance (and 40 percent buy life insurance) from Metropolitan Life.

2. **New Markets.** One example is the introduction of Mexican foods to geographic areas not familiar with them. Another is the

addition of breakfast menus to fast-food restaurants. Adding breakfasts not only increased profits by utilizing the outlets during hours when they had been closed, but also appealed to older people who had not frequented the chains before.

3. **New Efficiencies.** When computer stores first entered the market on a large scale, they usually offered computer hardware (and some software) only. ComputerLand was able to better serve—and satisfy—its customers by adding equipment maintenance and repair services, especially in areas that were not near computer manufacturers' outlets. These services turned ComputerLand into a one-stop center for most computer needs.

Continued growth

In 30 years, business-format franchising has grown from a handful of ice cream and hamburger stands into a multi-billion-dollar industry. While product and trade name franchising still accounts for nearly 75 percent of the dollars spent in franchised businesses, it must be kept in mind that this includes the sales of cars through licensed dealers, a considerably higher-ticket item than a Big Mac. In the last decade, business-format franchising has grown 15 percent faster than product licensing, in terms of both sales and number of establishments. Today, more than 2,000 business-format franchises operate in the U.S.—more than double the amount of just 10 years ago.

But, as they say, the past is prologue. Franchising has become one of the largest segments of American business, and is a proven way to expand a small local business into a large national or even international one. We have briefly examined what franchising is (and *isn't*), and how Ray Kroc made it work for his company. The next thing to examine is whether *your* business is ready for franchising.

Preparing For Expansion

2

For many companies, the problem of expansion is not unlike the problem of selecting a career for a student. On the one hand, everyone agrees that the matter requires considerable thought and study. But the tendency for most of us is to act on impulse, plunging in where opportunity presents itself.

The fact that you are reading this book suggests that you may be more deliberate than many fellow businesspeople in this respect. You have a desire to learn more than you already know about business expansion—or at least about one type of business expansion—before you make a decision.

We suggest that you review the various types of business expansion open to you—not simply franchising—and in this chapter we will try to assist you with that task. But before you consider the methods of expansion, we strongly recommend that you answer some critical questions about your own business. They are:

1. What are your goals?
2. What is the potential of your concept for expansion?
3. What are the financial and operational capabilities of your business?

Goals

If you own the business, you should first consider personal goals. Do you want to increase the value of your business in order to sell it in five years? Or to pass it down to your children? Or simply to respond to a challenge? Rarely are entrepreneurs we meet striving exclusively for monetary goals. They like winning, but they also like playing the game. They are people with a vision, and to realize that vision they will, if necessary, refinance their homes, endure the ridicule of their friends and the doubts of their family, and, of course, work long hours.

Assuming you want your business to grow, there is an important question to ask as you contemplate franchising: Are you willing to learn a new business? Because being a franchisor is different from being an entrepreneur-business owner. The demands are different. The relationship between you and your franchisees will be different from the relationship between you and your employees. In fact, it will be more like the relationship you have with your customers—or, as we have noted, with your spouse. And it's always possible that if you like your present role, you may not like the role you find yourself in as a franchisor.

By asking certain questions, you can also help to formulate your company's goals. For example:

• Is your company basically conservative or aggressive? Is it content with growing slowly and steadily, or is it poised for a more venturesome future?

• Will your company be able to exist at or near its present size for the forseeable future? Or does it need an increased market share to survive?

• Are your growth plans subject to the control of investors who may be less interested in growth and long-term capital gains than in uninterrupted income?

• Are your executives adaptable to new ideas and new ways of doing business?

The answers to these and similar questions will help you in the selection of an expansion alternative. They may even cause you to make changes in the company before undertaking *any* expansion program.

Potential

Now, before we go on, we would like you to stand back for a moment, metaphorically speaking, and think about your business. Suppose you were suddenly given all of the money you could possibly use for growth—as many millions of dollars as were required to create the maximum number of units the market would bear. Suppose, in addition, you could obtain all of the motivated people you would need as unit managers for this expansion. And finally, imagine that the market will hold still while you complete the program. Under these optimum, totally fantastic conditions, how many stores or other kinds of distribution outlets could you establish?

Before you answer, take a serious look at your business. If your company establishes multi-million dollar resort hotels, you will answer this question quite differently than if you build submarine-sandwich shops. How many outlets could you realistically have under the conditions described above? One hundred? Five hundred? Ten thousand? Whatever the answer, now you have a fair idea of your company's potential. And if your goal is to maximize that potential, at least you have a starting point for your expansion program.

Capabilities

Now, let's get back to reality. Assuming that your company has the potential for establishing, say, 500 units in the United States, and a lot more internationally, what are your capabilities at the present time for carrying out a program designed to achieve that potential? First, how much money do you have that can be devoted to expansion? Though some forms of expansion are less expensive than others, none that we know of are free. Do you have enough money to generate 500 units? If not, where will you get it?

Next, what are your operational strengths? Do you have the personnel you need to oversee your expansion? Can the people you do have grow with the company? Equally important, where and how will you find the people to manage those 500 distribution centers?

And now that we are being realistic, how much time do you have? Can you establish those 500 units—or enough of them to make a difference—before the market changes or before your competitors move in? You may regard your business concept as unique, or at least unusual. But in this age of information, "new" ideas can become obsolete before they're fully developed. At the Consumer Electronics Show each year, people from all over the world rent booth space to showcase their products. But some close their booths out of embarrassment on the first day when they discover that another company had the idea first and has developed it farther. It's not unusual for people who come to our office for a consultation to require us to sign a nondisclosure agreement, swear us to secrecy, and close the doors before revealing their franchise idea, the one "no one has ever heard of before." They are invariably astonished when we pull up on our electronic data base six other companies that are doing the same thing. The point is that time could be much more important to the growth of your business than you realize, and you may have less of it than you imagine.

Money...people...time. These three factors will largely determine the success or failure of your expansion program. They are therefore the three criteria against which you should measure any expansion program. Frankly, this book is about franchising because franchising is a way to expand quickly without large numbers of employees and with a limited amount of capital. But before we discuss in detail the advantages of franchising, let's look at other methods of expansion and see how they measure up to these criteria.

Company owned units

Adding company-owned units is the traditional method of expansion for retail-oriented businesses. Your company puts up all the money, maintains complete control of the expansion program, and retains all of the profits. Many companies never do anything else and are satisfied with their growth, however limited it may be. And company ownership is always limiting. For your business, the cost of adding a new unit might be $100,000 or it might be $5 million. The question is: How many of your units can your company fund in the space of a year, or in whatever window of opportunity exists? How much debt service can you afford? Or, conversely, how large a piece of your business are you willing to give up to achieve your expansion plans?

Obviously, the degree of expansion you can achieve will be limited by the amount of cash your company has at hand or can generate. In most cases, that limitation reduces expansion through company-owned units to a trickle. And in the process the window of opportunity can slam shut.

But there are other drawbacks to building company-owned units. One is people. Finding and keeping good managers is a difficult and time-consuming process. And it gets worse the farther you expand geographically. And although, as we have pointed out, you retain all the profits from each unit, you also have all of the contingent liability and responsibility for day-to-day management of each unit. It is possible, of course, to motivate managers by tying them into incentive programs based upon unit profitability. But sooner or later the sales volume of a unit tends to level off; whereupon the manager realizes he's not going to get rich and accepts the incentive simply as his due, a part of his salary. At that point, the incentive program for that manager loses its effect, and the manager's performance deteriorates or he/she begins looking elsewhere.

"Elsewhere" may lead to business ownership—either as independent owners or as franchisees. One of our clients, Jeff Haas, founded a submarine-sandwich chain called Bubba's Breakaway and built his franchise program in large part with his own former managers. Concentrating largely on college towns, Haas let it be known that Bubba's Breakaway had jobs for energetic young people who wanted to work their way into business ownership. The result: a steady stream of motivated managers who learn the ropes thoroughly working in company-owned stores and then acquires franchises of their own at relatively low cost.

How much profit can you expect from a store with a manager? And how long will it take (and at what level of risk) to recover your investment? If you're in a retail business and generating $300,000 in sales per year, the maximum is likely to be $30,000 to $45,000, against which must be placed all the costs of corporate supervision of that unit. Recovery of your investment could take three or four years, and there is always the chance of losing it entirely. By comparison, a franchised unit producing the same revenue may generate $15,000 per year in royalties. But in addition you receive an upfront franchise fee and you pay supervisory costs that are typically one-half to one-third lower than for a company-owned unit. And, of course, all the risk of ownership is borne by the franchisee.

Recently, executives of a large corporation came to us with the idea of franchising a chain of several hundred company-owned convenience stores. They complained that under management by employees the stores weren't doing as well as they should be. And they bemoaned the "incredible expense" of the cadre of supervisors required to oversee those employee managers. The company had looked at all of their options and decided that ownership at the unit level—franchising—was the only feasible possibility.

Indeed, the same decision has been made over and over again. During the late 1960s and early 1970s, McDonald's CEO Fred Turner decided to increase drastically the number of company-owned units, which stood at less than 10 percent in 1967. When the percentage of company-owned units reached one-third of all units, the company discovered it was having severe management problems. The decision was made to reduce the number of company-owned units to 25 percent, and by company policy that ceiling has been sustained. McDonald's is a gigantic company with enormous assets and an efficient supervisory superstructure in place nationally and internationally. If anyone can make a huge company-owned unit system work, McDonalds's can. But McDonald's learned from experience just how important motivated operators are at the unit level and how expensive the privilege of having total unit control can be.

Partnerships

Another alternative to franchising is the partnership. Partnerships can be tempting, especially when they bring needed cash to the business. And they can work well when the partners are capable and have temperaments that complement one another. But in our experience a successful partnership is very much the exception. Too many begin as friendships and end as disasters when the partners discover they have substantially different ideas about how the business should be run and what its goals should be. For the person dependent upon a business for his or her income, nothing is quite so frustrating as knowing your partner is running the business badly.

The general partner/limited partner arrangement avoids some hazards of the traditional partnership because each partner's role is clearly designated in advance. The general partner typically manages the business and raises necessary capital from the limited partners. In return, the limited partners receive the majority of the income as well as any tax advantages that may accrue to the business. However, current tax laws have minimized these advantages. Usually the general partner retains a small management fee as a percentage of gross sales and shares in the profits of the business, typically between 10 and 50 percent. There are costs involved in forming such a partnership, and in most states you can't simply advertise for partners without registering to sell a security. The regulations for selling securities at the state, and certainly at the federal, level are often more stringent than franchise regulations. So it can be very difficult and expensive to find good partners.

A partnership can give you the capital you need to expand, but you will also sacrifice a great deal of control. To make changes in the business, you will need the consent of your partners. If you cannot obtain timely consent, you could lose your ability to respond to changing market conditions. In a partnership, you also give up equity in your business. That may be too high a price to pay for capital; often it amounts to a permanent solution to a temporary problem.

Dealerships/distributorships

The type of expansion we have been discussing and will discuss throughout this book, of course, is enlargement of a company's distribution network (as opposed to increasing the size of existing facilities or growth through mergers and acquisitions). Traditionally, companies that distribute products have expanded by accessing existing channels of distribution, such as independent dealerships and/or distributorships. But many companies find such dealers or distributors difficult to motivate and impossible to control as they grow and prosper. This is especially true in highly competitive industries; dealers who offer a choice of products are likely to favor companies that offer large ad budgets and allowances, dating of invoices, and extensive name recognition over those that do not. If your company cannot compete in these areas, you may find your expansion program sputtering despite the superior advantages of your product or service. Besides, many large distributors and their personnel seem to prefer acting as order takers rather than vigorously promoting new products.

The franchising of dealerships is as old as franchising itself. Historically, however, the franchised dealer arrangement, though not as loose as independent dealer relationships, stops short of providing a business system. In recent years, some manufacturers have been converting dealers to franchising, offering as incentives an exclusive territory, extensive training, marketing support, and business systems that non-franchised dealers are not eligible to receive. Two companies that have discarded traditional dealership arrangements in favor of franchises of this type are Dahlberg, Inc., a Minnesota-based hearing aid company that operates more than 300 units known as Miracle-Ear Centers, and the Four Seasons Solar Products Corp., which manufactures greenhouses and solariums.

Dahlberg's conversion of dealers to franchisees took two tumultuous years and cost the company an estimated $5 million. But, by the time the first 250 Miracle-Ear Centers were opened in 1986—selling Dahlberg products only—the company realized a larger profit than it had ever experienced through dealership sales alone. While still distributing products through independent dealers, Dahlberg plans to convert to a solely franchised operation of more than 800 outlets by the early 1990s.

Four Seasons discovered the franchise advantage when they learned that most of their independent dealers regarded them as "just another supplier" of greenhouse-style room additons. These dealers devoted little effort to selling their line and consequently produced few sales. A few productive dealers, however, promoted the line aggressively, and were so enthusiastic about the resulting sales volume that they started to demand exclusive territories so they could afford to spend full time on the line. As a result, Four Seasons ended their dealership agreements and started distributing solely through franchisees. Today, they have 200 greenhouse design centers across the country, marketing, selling, and installing their products. By franchising, Four Seasons has achieved an added measure of control over their "sales force," including a guarantee of undivided loyalty to their products.

Licensing

Some companies expand through licensing, a term often used interchangeably, albeit mistakenly, with franchising. All franchises contain at least one license, but not every license is a franchise. Consider the following definition of franchising and note how broad and encompassing it is compared to the mere granting of a license:

Franchising is a method of doing business by which an individual or company is granted the right to offer, sell, or distribute goods or services under a marketing plan or system prescribed by the franchisor and substantially associated with the franchisor's trademark, name, logo, or advertising.

In a classic licensing arrangement, the licensor merely gives the licensee the right to use the licensor's name on a product, business, or formula without substantially regulating how the licensee conducts his or her business. Coca-Cola, for example, may allow a manufacturer to put the Coca-Cola name and symbol on t-shirts, but Coca-Cola doesn't prescribe how the manufacturer will make, distribute, or market the t-shirts.

Licensing is a multi-billion-dollar industry, and one that companies can enter for relatively little cost. And the returns can be phenomenal—in a single year, designers such as Bill Blass, Pierre Cardin, and Yves Saint Laurent have made millions of dollars by licensing their names. Hamilton Projects, Inc., a licensing consulting firm that has handled such accounts as the Statue of Liberty, Harley Davidson, the Brooklyn Bridge, Coca-Cola, and numerous sports and cartoon figures, identifies three major reasons why businesses enter into licensing arrangements:

1. To protect their trademark in a number of different product categories.
2. To enhance the visibility that trademark would receive.
3. To generate additional revenues in the form of royalty payments. (A typical arrangement might bring a company a royalty of 5 percent of the wholesale price of any product bearing the licensor's name or trademark. The only real risk is that the name might be used on poorly-made products and tarnish the company's image.)

If you're looking at licensing, the business questions you have to ask yourself are: Can I really allow a licensee to use my name without controlling his whole system of operation? Could it materially affect the quality of the goods and services sold under my name? If you decide that for your business to expand successfully your licensee must operate his business in a prescribed way, if the licensee pays you more than $500 during the first six months of your relationship, and if you are willing to let him use your name (even if you don't require him to do so), you have probably sold a franchise. You may, of course, continue to call it a license, and some franchisors prefer the word "license" to the word "franchise." Just be sure, however, that if you sell such "licenses" you are conforming to the franchise laws.

Sales representatives

Companies, especially manufacturers, can grow by creating sales forces of employees or by hiring independent contractors to act as their sales representatives. This is the old-line, traditional system of maintaining presences and service far from a corporate headquarters. Before the advent of MBAs, many eventual corporate leaders including franchising legends such as Ray Kroc and Jules Lederer, cut their business teeth as sales representatives.

But company sales forces are enormously expensive to operate. Good sales representatives are difficult to find, train, motivate, compensate, and retain. And the larger and more diffused the sales force becomes, the more severe all of these problems can be. The fact is that the best salespeople tend to be "lone rangers." They rarely integrate well into a company culture. Continental Data Systems of Pennsylvania is one of an increasing number of companies that are turning to franchising to find capable salespeople. A value-added reseller of IBM computer hardware and software for the medical and legal professions, Continental Data Systems sold 25 franchise sales territories in its first year. Not only is Continental Data Systems relieved of the necessity to hire a sales force, they can penetrate markets that the company might not otherwise have been able to afford to enter and collect a fee at the same time. The franchise owner is motivated by his or her own investment, and, like an employee (but unlike an independent distributor), works full time to promote Continental Data Systems' products.

Cooperative associations

Some independent businesses similar in nature have formed cooperative associations for the purpose of buying and advertising together. Best Western hotels and Ace Hardware stores are examples that come quickly to mind. Both organizations consist entirely of independently-owned businesses that adopt the Best Western or Ace Hardware name and contribute to a central organization that provides advertising and buying services for the members but does not exercise control over them. Aside from the difficulty of forming such chains, there are two obvious disadvantages to cooperative associations. First, while they may help to strengthen individual units or existing chains that join the association, they are not designed to foster unit growth by the independent owners. Second, because in cooperatives the central governing authority is given power by the individual members, rather than the reverse, the organization's power is severely limited. In contrast, a franchisor can introduce new concepts and make them part of the operating procedures of the entire franchise; associations that function as one-member, one-vote democracies, such as Ace Hardware, have much greater difficulty making and implementing changes.

Sale of consulting services

Some owners of successful businesses sell their expertise to others who want to establish similar businesses—especially buyers who are outside of their geographic area and, therefore, are not direct competitors. In a sense, this can be called an alternative way of expansion because it can be a source of revenue. And although it does not involve much risk on the part of the "consultant" (except insofar as encouraging competitors can be called risk), the rewards are extremely limited. Our clients Alan and Richard Levine, owners of The Baby's Room (a children's furniture franchise in Chicago with sales in excess of $25 million per year), sold their services in this manner for some time. Then, as they watched their "students" prosper using the business system they invented, they realized that they were literally giving away the store. Today, their franchisees are paying them a good deal more for the same advice.

As you might expect, all of the above leads to the question: What is the best way to expand? For many of our readers the answer will be found in the next chapter.

The Franchise Advantage

We have shown you the alternatives to franchising partly as a way of explaining what franchising is and partly to reveal why franchising has become the most popular form of business expansion in the twentieth century. But let's examine in greater detail both the pros and the cons of franchising.

The pros

Capital

As we've stated, franchising is a method of expansion that enables a business to expand rapidly with minimum capital. All other expansion methods require that either you spend existing capital or borrow it. Analysts in our firm speak with more than 7,000 business owners and managers a year, yet you'd be astonished how few of their companies have large amounts of capital. They've been busy plowing their money back into their businesses in order to improve them.

Where, then, do successful businesses get money to expand? Some businesses elect to sell shares of stock to obtain money, and in turn relinquish a certain amount of autonomy and control. Others go to the bank. But the bank wants collateral; and there's only so much collateral in any business. Your company's most valuable assets—you and your people—walk out of the door every night.

We know of only one efficient way to expand without giving up control of either your business or its assets: by selling franchises. We should make it clear, however, that—at least in the beginning—the money you get for the sales themselves will usually do little more than pay your expenses for setting up a franchise program and training your franchisees (although that, frankly, is quite a lot). And, unless you buy real estate and lease it to your franchisees (which would require capital), you really won't own any part of their businesses. Nevertheless, a chain of franchised establishments (or an army of franchised sales reps or distributors) using your name and paying ongoing royalties to you certainly, in our opinion, constitutes a form of capital.

Motivated "managers"

As every business owner knows, good managers are hard to find. And once you have found them and trained them at considerable expense, they aren't easy to keep. Even a manager on the incentive system doesn't actually own anything. Nothing really binds him to his job.

The franchisee, first and foremost, is not an employee. He buys with his own money the rights to own and operate a business similar to the one you have created. And, in the tradition of business ownership, the franchisee is at risk. He or she must commit time and energy, as well as capital, to its success.

You must, of course, train a franchisee even more extensively than you would a manager. But once trained, as we noted earlier, a franchisee can be far less rigorously supervised than an employee. Your role in the day-to-day operation of the franchisee's business is more that of a grandparent than a parent. You're there when needed for advice and counsel, but you don't have the day-to-day responsibility for direct management.

Some businesses that our company has helped to franchise had already established several company-owned units before they came to us. Often, these companies sell off some of their units to managers who become their first franchisees, thus engendering good feelings among employees throughout their company—while simultaneously creating a pool of satisfied franchise owners.

In general, motivated manager-owners can be beneficial to a franchisor in each of the following three areas:

1. Image. At the local level, the franchisee is a very visible member of a community or neighborhood. A local franchisee generally represents a higher level of community commitment and involvement with customers than does an absentee owner.

2. Profitability. With a franchisee involved in the hands-on operation of a franchise, labor costs can be kept down, allowing a unit to be profitable with a smaller population base (and possibly with lower sales levels) than other units may require.

3. Efficiency. Local owner-managers can usually operate their units with more efficiency and less bureaucracy than a company-run unit. The franchisee is also more attuned to changes his specific unit may need to adapt to his community.

Domino's Pizza has created satisfied franchisees in a slightly different way, especially in college towns. Domino's employs students part-time while at school and moves them quickly into the role of manager. At the end of a year, if the student-managers do well, Domino's allows them to become franchise owners. If, at that point, they cannot come up with the $80,000 to $110,000 to open their own unit, Domino's assists them in obtaining financing, requiring however that the franchisee maintain at least 51 percent of ownership regardless of who supplies the money. By the end of the year, these young managers have been thoroughly trained in the Domino's system and know exactly what they're getting into.

Rapid expansion

Let's assume that you have an unusual concept—one you've tried and tested locally but that has not been exploited by any other company nationally. Or let's suppose another company has made your concept work in some other region of the country and you are concerned that they will move in to compete against you in your region. Franchising is the one expansion system that enables the small or medium-sized entrepreneur to become the dominant force in a market by being first in the market. Because large amounts of capital are not required by the franchisor, big-spending giant corporations find it not so easy to wait until a company has "softened up" the market before moving in and taking over. On the contrary, in franchising, a head start by anyone is extremely significant. A successful franchise program attracts prospective franchisees like a gold strike attracts miners. As the most successful franchises grow, the problem becomes less one of "selling" franchises than of separating qualified from unqualified applicants.

Franchising, then, can enable you to saturate an existing market and penetrate new markets as well. And as your franchise grows you can, if you desire, use earned revenues to build additional company-owned units, particularly in areas where you feel you need market saturation to limit your competitor's access to that market.

Buying power

As your franchise grows, collective buying power can become a significant advantage. Everything from equipment to inventory can be purchased by franchisees from approved suppliers at group discounts. In fact, for franchisees in product businesses, the savings resulting from collective buying often surpass the royalty fees they pay. If the franchisee can reduce his or her cost of goods by 10 or 20 percent, that amount goes straight to the bottom line. There are collective buying advantages for a service-oriented business, too, including better equipment that helps the franchisee do the job faster, less expensively, and more efficiently. As a franchisor, you may want to devote some portion of your income to developing new technology, new products, or new systems that will benefit your franchisees collectively.

Another collective-buying advantage of franchising is the ability to pool funds for advertising and public relations programs. We referred earlier to the importance of name recognition in business. The cumulative effect of advertising—especially TV advertising—by big companies has put a virtual end in certain areas to direct competition by small businesses against giants with names that are household words. Thirty years ago in the United States small restaurants with names like "Joe's Hamburgers" abounded. (Many were referred to appropriately as "greasy spoons.") Today, in most large cities, only the big three (McDonald's, Burger King, Wendy's) make low-priced, traditional hamburgers their principal menu items. These days, if you want to get into the low-priced hamburger game, you have to do something different, such as make 'em tiny (White Castle) or serve them to motorists at double drive-thru units (Beefy's). What created this environment? Franchising and television advertising. It's an enormously powerful one-two punch.

Of course, rarely is a new franchise able to afford network television. But even chains with a few units can make use of local television. In some cases, cable offers excellent low-cost exposure in particular markets.

Where do franchise advertising dollars come from? Usually from franchisees. Take McDonald's, for example. In 1986, McDonald's spent approximately $525 million for advertising, second only to Procter and Gamble. Most of that money was contributed by franchisees. The average annual gross sales for a

McDonald's unit in 1986 was $1.3 million. Four percent of that amount was collected for advertising, or about $52,000 annually. That is not an insubstantial amount for a single fast-food restaurant. But multiply $52,000 times 6,000 or more franchised stores, add the same contributions from company-owned stores and you see clearly how much more effective the advertising allotment of a McDonald's is than a similar amount spent by a non-affiliated restaurant. By spending $52,000, a single McDonald's unit has the power to obtain year-round television advertising of the highest quality in its market. In a large city, that amount could be exhausted on television by an independent in a few days, even if spent judiciously.

Of course, buying power of all kinds can accrue to any chain—franchised or non-franchised. But the chain that grows fastest is likely to be the chain that benefits most from collective buying. And franchised chains, as we have seen, tend to grow bigger, faster.

Revenue

There is not much point to expanding through franchising or any other method unless at least one of your goals is financial. So, it must be asked, how well does franchising fare as a source of revenue for the franchisor?

As we have shown, expansion through company-owned units does ensure that all profit from a given unit goes to the company. On the other hand, all the losses and capital investment of a company-owned unit must be borne by the company as well. In contrast, most franchisors have, strictly speaking, nothing to do with profits or losses of individual units. If a franchisee makes a lot of money, wonderful. The franchisor, however, does not share in that gain, as such. Nor does the franchisor share in any losses the franchisee may incur because the franchisees usually pay royalties on gross sales, not profits. (This is not to imply, of course, that if your franchisees are unsuccessful you will continue to derive revenue from them for very long. If a franchise fails, as some do, the owner will stop paying you.)

Franchisors can derive revenue from six sources:
1. Initial franchise fee
2. Royalties
3. Advertising fees
4. Sales of products to franchisees
5. Sales of additional services to franchisees
6. Rental of property

We have spoken of advertising already. It is not, strictly speaking, a profit center for a franchisor. The other five sources of revenue, however, can be.

The initial franchise fee is a one-time admission fee to the franchise program. It covers, to at least some degree, your cost of becoming a franchisor, franchise marketing, training the franchisee, site selection assistance, sales commission, and start-up assistance. It should, in addition, help to offset the losses you incur until the franchisee's royalty payments exceed your support costs. Such fees range from as little as $10,000 for a Kentucky Fried Chicken franchise (supposing you were able to secure one of these highly-sought units) to as much as $75,000 for a ComputerLand franchise.

Ongoing income is derived by the franchisor from the royalty, usually a percentage of gross sales agreed to in the franchise agreement that can range from four percent in a low-margin business to 20 percent in a high-margin, low-volume service business. It is the royalty that must support the franchisor's ongoing services to his franchisees. Selecting the right royalty is important, but royalties that are too low and do not permit a franchisor to provide adequate services can be as dangerous to a franchise program as royalties that later prove too high or unfair. High royalties can be lowered; low royalties can rarely be raised.

Products and services can be sold to franchisees at your option and can have a significant impact upon your income. However, we generally recommend that franchisors limit these sales to products closely identified with the business itself and not easily obtained at comparable price and quality elsewhere. On the other hand, special services, such as accounting or payroll management, not only assist the franchisees but help the franchisor to accurately monitor their operations. Such tailor-made services can be an excellent buy for the franchisee. It may also be possible, if you wish, to lease real estate or equipment to your franchisees, although (generally speaking) such activity is better left to seasoned franchisors.

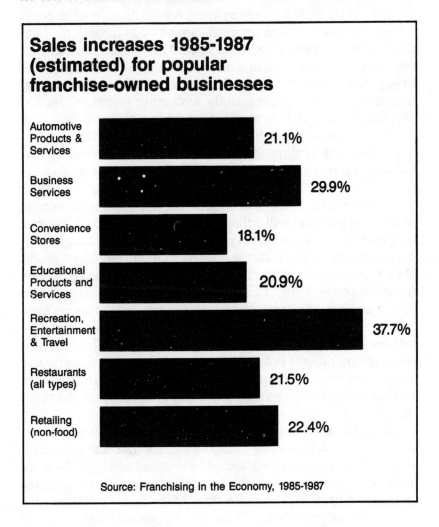

Sales increases 1985-1987 (estimated) for popular franchise-owned businesses

Automotive Products & Services — 21.1%

Business Services — 29.9%

Convenience Stores — 18.1%

Educational Products and Services — 20.9%

Recreation, Entertainment & Travel — 37.7%

Restaurants (all types) — 21.5%

Retailing (non-food) — 22.4%

Source: Franchising in the Economy, 1985-1987

The Hair Performers franchise, founded by John Amico, has created numerous profit centers over the years. Amico began opening hair salons in the 1970s to capitalize on the unisex phenomenon. He became a franchisor partly as an alternative to giving people free advice about starting their own hair salons and partly because many of his students were prospective franchisees. As the Hair Performers grew, Amico discovered he could sell private-label hair and personal-care products through his franchises, offering a commission on sales to the franchisees and their employees. Understand that Amico doesn't require his franchisees to buy these products, but he does provide them at a substantial discount, competing successfully with other suppliers. He has also been able to sell some of his products outside the franchise system, and now has a full-scale manufacturing plant.

Rudimentary arithmetic will show how, if a franchise grows quickly, the revenue can add up. However, we repeat: Success in franchising is, in the long run, predicated on the success of your franchisees. If the franchisees are not successful, sooner or later the program will collapse. If they are successful, the rate of franchise sales can be very rapid indeed. So, although franchisor income is not directly connected with franchisee profitability, the franchise program itself is ultimately dependent upon franchisee profitability. One client of ours, Merle Harmon's Fan Fair, a company that sells team-oriented products to sports fans, sold 10 franchises in its first year—placing all in regional malls— and decided that number was enough for awhile. They consolidated for six months before rolling out an even more aggressive expansion program. Another client, Beefy's, a double drive-thru hamburger operation, sold 23 franchises in its first year and never looked back.

As quickly as a franchise can expand by selling individual units, such expansion is nothing compared to the rate some franchisors have achieved through area development and subfranchisor sales. We'll say more about this later, but Century 21 did not grow from one unit in 1971 to more than 7,500 units in 1979 by selling individual franchises. This rate of growth was achieved primarily by selling the rights to sell individual franchises to sub-franchisors throughout the United States.

Locations

If yours is the kind of business that places a high value on locations, franchising can give you the muscle you need to make mall owners and developers listen. The number of malls is finite—and, indeed, so also is the number of openings for any given business in any given mall. Merle Harmon's Fan Fair gets many of its best franchise prospects from mall developers who have seen how well the stores do.

Flexibility

Franchising adapts remarkably well to a variety of corporate situations, structures, and goals. Although the classical picture of a franchisor is one of a small company with limited financial resources, which relies on its franchisees to provide the startup capital, construct units, hire employees, and manage daily operations, some highly successful franchisors have found it profitable to assume some or all of these functions themselves—for a fee.

Convenience store franchisors such as Southland Corporation (7-Eleven), for example, often sell individual franchisees a "turnkey" package in which the franchisor acquires the property or signs the lease, constructs the unit, purchases and installs the equipment, and even supplies the inventory. The franchisee in essence "buys himself a job," paying a monthly percentage of his volume (in addition to his franchise royalty) to cover unit rent and lease payments. Although requiring Southland to make a heavier capital investment than the typical franchise arrangement would, this program gives them another source of revenue, as well as a means to control locations and build their asset base. (It also allows them to tap a fertile source of dedicated unit management: owner/operators who otherwise couldn't afford the start-up costs.)

McDonald's is another prime example of a franchisor which profits from returns on its real estate holdings. While only 25 percent of their units are company-owned, McDonald's owns or controls 60 percent of the real estate on which their U.S. units stand. In fact, they receive more revenues from leases than they do from franchise royalties.

Franchisors who have more capital to invest, then, can derive even better returns from franchising while still enjoying the benefits of dedicated owner/operators handling local management. Franchising can also be flexible in the other direction. If you're short on capital but long on management ability, you can let your franchisees put up all the capital, but offer your services to manage the units. Merle Harmon's Fan Fair, among others, has found this approach to be an excellent means to attract multiple-unit investors who have the funds and see the potential of their concept but don't have the time, the experience, or the desire to oversee day-to-day management.

Such "management contracts" typically allow the management company to share in the profits—over and above, of course, the normal percentage of gross revenues paid as royalty to the franchisor. These arrangments are quite common in the hotel industry, as well. Our client, Omni Hotels, for example, maintains a large hotel management staff which runs properties for a variety of absentee owner/investors all over the country.

So, in addition to being an efficient way for small companies to grow quickly, a franchise system can also be highly productive for firms with more resources—and expectations of even better returns.

Exit strategy

One other advantage of franchising worth mentioning is the added value a franchise program can give to a company in the business marketplace. Between 1984 and 1987, eight of our franchisor clients were acquired by other companies. Four of the eight were bought and quietly absorbed by competitors. For example, Crispy

Chick, an Alabama-based, 37-unit chain of fast food chicken restaurants, was purchased by Church's Fried Chicken. Two clients retained their names, though not precisely the same management. Cassano's Pizza, a well-known company in the Dayton area, had repositioned itself with a delivery and carryout concept and was selling multi-unit territories when Greyhound Food Management, Inc. made an attractive offer to its founder, Vic Cassano. Silk Plants, Etc., a Chicago-based chain, after getting off to a rapid start (selling 30 franchises in its first year), was sold to Ozite Corporation. In both cases, the buyer was better qualified financially than the original owner to take the franchise national. But in every case, franchising had made the business a more valuable asset than it had been before.

The Cons

For all of its extraordinary advantages, franchising isn't perfect and doesn't work for every business. The disadvantages of franchising must also be considered by any business contemplating expansion.

Loss of control

The biggest single drawback to franchising is loss of control. By giving up control of the operating units to franchisees, the franchisor takes two risks. His first, and not necessarily highest, risk is that the franchisees will be unable to operate the business as he has operated it, that the complexities of the business are such that it cannot be taught to a franchisee within an acceptable period of time. More and more, this obstacle is being overcome by extensive training programs employed by such companies as Domino's and McDonald's and by offering unit management as an available service (as described above). But the fact is that the day-to-day operation of most retail businesses can be taught very quickly. Rarely do franchisors train franchisees for longer than 30 days. One or two weeks is far more common, although not always enough time, in our opinion.

The second risk is that the franchisor will find loss of control difficult to accept. It's sometimes difficult for an entrepreneur who has created a business and perfected it to turn loose the reins. Some business owners who say they want to be less involved in day-to-day operations find stepping aside extremely difficult when the time comes. As owner, you can tell the manager to change the prices, change the layout, change the inventory, even change the tie he's wearing that day if you don't like it. As franchisor, you must suggest, motivate, and persuade, not command. Your franchisee doesn't fire very easily. Franchising is, as we have noted, like marriage—easy to get into, hard to get out of.

Of course, the fact is that franchising as a business can be as interesting as any other and, if power and authority turn you on, can be more rewarding than most. But it requires different skills than those you needed to start your existing business. Instead of risk-taking and drive, a franchisor needs to master the art of diplomacy, become a good listener, and learn to speak in public.

Another aspect of losing control over each unit—and a possible point of contention—is the problem of prices and profit vs. total sales. Are the franchisee's retail prices too high, driving customers to competitors? Or are the prices too low, crippling the franchisee's profits and the franchisor's royalty? The franchisee's goal is to maximize profit, but the franchisor's goal—based on royalty percentages—is maximum *sales* per unit. Therefore, franchisees may resist price, equipment, or labor changes that they perceive to be increasing total sales but not profits.

Conflicts and lawsuits

Potential conflicts and lawsuits are, indeed, another disadvantage of franchising, although most franchisors encounter few problems of this kind so long as their franchisees are successful. Trouble comes when they are not. An investment banker friend recently said, "All investors are sophisticated until they lose money." The same is true with your franchisees, who claim that they will never sue you—until they lose money. At that point, you are potentially open to claims of fraud, misrepresentation, inadequate training, and so forth. The legal costs of defending yourself against such accusations can be significant.

On the other hand, let's be realistic. If you borrow money to expand and the business fails, your lender is likely to either sue you or claim the collateral you pledged. If you have sold equity in your company to investors and fail to meet your projections, you may lose control of your company, lose your job as CEO, and perhaps be sued for fraud and misrepresentation as well. In franchising, you have the motivation of the owner-manager working to prevent failure. Neither your banker nor your equity investor will be on the firing line working to help your franchise succeed.

Moreover, according to the U.S. Department of Commerce, the failure rate for franchisees is only five percent, and the key to avoiding conflicts and litigation is to select the proper franchisees to begin with, give them adequate training and support, manage the franchise program properly, sustain a good franchisee relationship, and look out for changes in the industry or in the economy that could affect your business. Creating a successful franchise can be an even greater challenge than creating the business that made you a franchisor.

Finding qualified franchisees

Successful franchisees are the backbone of any franchise program, but the important first steps are to attract and then sign up franchisees with the best potential for success. Franchisees must be financially able to bear the start-up costs of the franchise unit. But a high initial investment can scare off some otherwise qualified franchisees. So can a business that is perceived as complex, such as a business-service franchise. Another point to consider is that today, with thousands of franchise opportunities available, franchisors must, in effect, compete against each other for the most savvy franchisees.

Profitability per unit

As noted earlier, total receipt of unit profits in a company-owned business is exchanged in franchising for a royalty, usually a percentage of gross sales. In successful units, that percentage will be far lower than the unit's total profit. This disadvantage, of course, must be weighed against franchising's many advantages, including minimal risk of capital by the franchisor, rapid expansion potential, and collective buying power.

Changing markets

If franchisors do not keep current with changes in the marketplace or in their industry, they may find themselves left behind or even out of business. During its early years as the computer retailer market-leader, ComputerLand charged its franchisees a royalty of eight percent. While this was higher than competitors' royalty rates, the franchisees by and large did not mind, because ComputerLand's buying power and quantity discounts enabled them to make sufficient profits. When the personal computer industry changed in the early 1980s, more manufacturers and dealers emerged, ComputerLand's clout diminished, and margins shrank. However, ComputerLand kept on charging its franchisees an eight-percent royalty. Facing both franchisee failures and a threatened "revolt" from a large number of its franchisees, ComputerLand was forced to reduce its royalty to six percent and endure a loss in franchisor revenue.

Unmanageable growth

For some people, building a franchise can be almost too easy. Even with all the laws that protect prospective franchisees, some franchisors prove to be far better sellers of franchises than business operators. When a franchisor creates a monster beyond his capacity to manage, the fall can be sudden and dramatic.

Command Performance hair salons was a classic example of this type of franchise failure. The original Command Performance franchisor sold and promoted the franchise very effectively, but was less effective as a manager, and did not have the needed support programs in place. In addition, rental payments made by franchisees on units owned by the company were used to fund the marketing program, and when the system ultimately went bankrupt, many franchisees found themselves evicted. At that point, the 600 Command Performance franchisees engaged our firm to explore possible solutions. We suggested three options: 1. Buy the company out of its bankruptcy; 2. Form a new company; 3. Join forces with another existing franchisor. The franchisees chose the third and linked up with a franchisor in a different industry, Docktor Pet Centers, Inc., under the direction of Carl M. Youngman and Leslie Charm, who have successfully turned the company around and made it profitable.

D'Lites of America, Inc., is another example of a company that grew too fast. D'Lites units served low-fat, low-calorie hamburgers, sandwiches, and salads in a fast-food setting, seemingly a winning idea given Americans' obsession with health and weight-loss. In four years, D'Lites opened 86 restaurants, 63 of them sold to franchisees, yet in 1985 losses were phenomenal, with some franchisees losing as much as $1 million on their units. Several reasons have been cited for the franchise's failure—that big chains added lighter menus and salad bars, that new franchisees lacked sufficient restaurant experience, and that the franchisor provided inadequate support in training and marketing. The future that looked so promising to the franchisees and to D'Lites management failed to materialize. In addition, the protections and incentives that certain franchisees, notably the company's founder and its president, received in the operation of their units adversely affected the morale of the other franchisees and drained away capital that could have been used to promote D'Lites more aggressively to consumers.

There are ways, of course, to keep growth through franchising manageable. One is to sell franchises within an easily serviceable geographic area until you have built the kind of organization that can handle more rapid expansion. Another is to sell a limited number of franchises—at least in the early stages. The key to real success in franchising is to recognize that only by building a company in which franchisees succeed can you be truly successful. And if we repeat this more than once during the course of this book, it's because history shows it needs repeating.

The bottom line

The fact remains that despite occasional spectacular failures—and, to be sure, some less spectacular failures—franchising enjoys a phenomenal success record. As we have noted, the U.S. Department of Commerce assesses the failure rate for franchisees as a minuscule five percent or less per year, while estimates of failures of new businesses range as high as 65 to 90 percent. Franchisor failures are also low. In 1985, 46 franchisors with a total of 1,463 units failed. Sales by franchisees in this group represented only one-tenth of one percent of total business-format franchising sales.

This incredible record does not prevent critics finding other, less tangible "disadvantages" to franchising. We have noted that some say, for example, that because franchising relies on uniformity and consistency, it promotes mediocrity and stifles individuality. However, there is no reason to assume that because a business or a product is consistent and reliable, it is necessarily mediocre. In fact, if that were the case, its chances for success would be reduced, since consumers look for the best value for their dollar. Nor does the franchising system stifle creativity. It encourages entrepreneurs to make their ideas reality and to allow other people who may be less willing to take such risks to share in their success. This ties in with another criticism of franchising—that it puts small businesses, the mom-and-pop operations, out of business. In reality, it does just the opposite. The moms-and-pops whose grocery stores went out of business have been replaced by the same kinds of people who now own 7-Elevens, am/pm mini markets, or Convenient Food Marts, which are more profitable, better organized, and more easily resold than the corner grocery ever was.

How many businesses could a novice enter into with an investment of less than $75,000, or less than $50,000, and with a training period of a week or two, yet feel secure in having a 95 percent chance of success? *Venture* magazine's 1986 listing of the top 100 franchisors shows 42 franchises that require a total investment of less than $75,000; 35 of those require less than $50,000. And they're all growing at phenomenal rates because they give individuals the chance to own their own businesses, with the security of having a company with a proven record to back them up.

Franchising is the American Dream, with a safety net. It's the most effective merger of large-organization efficiency with small-entrepreneur motivation ever devised. Not every successful business should franchise, but given the proper situation and concept, it can be an extraordinary wealth-producing system for the business that is franchisable.

Is Your Business Franchisable?

Franchising is full of bright new ideas that give one pause to stop and wonder, "Now, why didn't I think of that?" It also is full of adroit imitators—companies successfully doing business in a field that someone else has pioneered. As long as a business meets the criteria of franchisability (more about which, shortly), there is room both for the creative entrepreneur and the clever copy-cat. And then there's a blend of the two, the discoverer of that magical "niche." The businessperson who has unearthed and filled a niche can get a franchise off to a flying start.

These days, when people look at the hamburger segment of the fast-food market, they talk of the Big Three—McDonald's, Burger King, and Wendy's. Is there room for a big fourth? It doesn't seem likely, but you can't rule it out. When Wendy's came along in 1969, it was pretty much the new kid on the block. McDonald's already had been franchising for 14 years, Burger

King for 11 years. Many industry observers were saying that the Big Two had the marketplace pretty well sewed up. Wendy's proved them wrong, and it did it by, among other things, carving out a niche for itself.

Wendy's found its niche by targeting young adults, a key segment of an otherwise crowded marketplace. It did it by offering a larger hamburger made of high-quality beef, by adding chili to its menu to appeal to adult palates, by providing a pleasing "old fashioned" decor, and by offering a level of service aimed to please older customers, with help clearing off tables rather than customers disposing of their own debris. The marketing strategy worked. Within 10 years Wendy's was drawing 82 percent of its customers from the 25-plus population, in contrast to McDonald's which then was generating 35 percent of its revenues from the under-19 market. Wendy's hadn't so much horned in on an existing market as created a new one—much to the relief of other hamburger chains. The rest, as they say, is history. By the mid-80s, the scorecard read: McDonald's 8,300 units, Burger King 4,300 units, Wendy's 3,300 units.

Finding a niche, then, is one measure of potential franchisability. Certainly there are lots of niches filled by enterprising franchises—and lots more waiting to be exploited. Drive down Main Street, U.S.A., and you'll see clones of successful businesses plying the consumer with everything from art frames to zinnias. In fact, the average American would be hard-pressed to get through a day without coming into contact with a franchise. They have become ubiquitous for the simple reason that nearly any kind of business is franchisable. Franchises have been successful in selling everything from donuts to dentures, hearing aids to hardware, wallpaper to waffles. They have also proven successful in selling services ranging from automotive repairs to office cleaning. We've seen recently that professional affiliations can be candidates for franchising as well. Dental offices, accounting practices, insurance brokerages, and surgical centers are just a few of the franchise offerings in today's market.

Opportunities

The U.S. Department of Commerce's yearly *Franchise Opportunities Handbook* contains hundreds of pages of listings describing the myriad products and services offered in franchising. We've listed a few of the many categories below, including a sampling of the businesses they encompass, and for each type of business there may be dozens of franchisors.

**Automotive Products
  and Services**
Alarms
Batteries
Brakes
Alignment
Paint Protection
Vinyl Roofs
Radiators
Accessories
Tires
Mufflers
Transmissions
Detailing
Washing
Lubrication
Parts
Paint
Stereo
Sun Screens
Rustproofing
Upholstery
Air Conditioning
Fuel Systems

Auto/Trailer Rentals
Cars

Trucks
Vans
Trailers

Beauty Salons & Supplies

Business Aids/Services
Advertising
Videotaping
Loan Packaging
Agricultural Consulting
Limousines
Air Freight
Cemetery Management
Energy Systems
Barter Services
Résumés
Business Consultants
Credit Checks
Packaging
Computerized Billing
Travel
Publishing
Legal Advice
Mail Forwarding
Housing Inspections
Income Tax Preparation
Franchise Consulting
Long Distance Calling

Accounting
Collection Services
Singing Telegrams
Newsletters
Real Estate Management
Business Brokers
Pension Plans
Direct Mail Marketing

Campgrounds
Tents
Cars/RVs

**Children's
  Products/Services**
Furniture
Clothing
Education

Clothing
Athletic Wear
Formal Wear
Lingerie
Bridal Gowns
T-shirts
Casual Clothes
Maternity

**Construction/Remodeling
  Materials & Services**
Bathrooms
Concrete
Chimneys
Closets
Energy Conservation
Gutters
Geodesic Domes

Log Homes
Greenhouses
Kitchens
Sliding Doors
Repairs
Steel Buildings
Drains
Porcelain
Waterproofing
Painting
Windows

Cosmetics/Toiletries
Aloe
Cologne
Skin Care
Make-Up
Nail Care

Dental Centers

Drug Stores

Educational Products/Services
Modeling
Early Learning
Birth Preparation
Recording Studio Training
College Preparatory
Computer Centers
Driving Schools
Hotel Schools
Travel Training
Speed Reading
Remedial Reading

Sales Training
Banking Careers
Soap Opera Techniques
Exercise
Day Care

Employment Services
Temporary
Specialized by Field
Professional
Permanent Placements

Equipment Rentals

Food
Donuts
Groceries
Bakeries
Coffee
Cheese
Meat
Cookies
Delicatessens
Pizza
Health Food
Sandwiches
Ice Cream
Yogurt
Popcorn
Beverages
Vitamins
Pancakes
Waffles
Pretzels
Hamburgers

Bagels
Chicken
Mexican Food
Hot Dogs
Sausage
Barbecue
Chinese Food
Oranges
Pasta
Steak
Wine
Ribs

Health Aids
Diet Control
Exercise
Home Health Care
Aerobics
First Aid
Skin Care
Hearing Aids

Home Furnishings
   Retail/Repair/Services
Carpet
Carpet Cleaning
Decorating
Furniture
Beds
Water Purification
Bedding
Wallpaper
Windows
Paint

Insurance

**Laundry/Dry Cleaning
Services**

**Lawn & Garden Supplies
& Services**

**Maid Services/Home
Cleaning/Party Serving**

**Maintenance—Cleaning/
Sanitation Services
& Supplies**

Hotels & Motels

Optical Products/Services

Pet Centers

Printing
Photocopies
Typesetting
Business Cards

Real Estate

**Recreation, Entertainment,
Travel—Supplies
& Services**
Travel Agencies
Canoe Outfitters
Batting Range
Flight Simulation
Pool Halls
Mobile Disc Jockeys
Miniature Golf
Go-Karts
Martial Arts

**Computer Supplies
& Services**

Florists

Miscellaneous Retailing

Art Supplies
Bookstores
Bath Shops
Balloons
Tapes & Records
Cooking Supplies
Cutlery
Bird Feeders
Cameras
Watch Bands
Televisions
Clocks
Film Processing
Candles
Photos
Foreign Imports
Tobacco
Videos
Used Clothing
Jewelry
Security Systems
Swimming Pools
Tools and Hardware
Vending Machines

Miscellaneous Services
Hot Tubs
Balloon Bouquets
Suntans
Oxygen Therapy
Management Consulting
Babysitting
Wedding Planning
Moving
Dating
Fire Protection

Is franchising for everyone?

At first glance, looking at the enormous variety of franchised businesses, it would seem that the scope of franchising is broad enough to work for virtually any kind of business. Yet this is not so. Just because someone is successfully franchising a sandwich shop, it doesn't mean that *your* particular sandwich shop is franchisable—or, indeed, that you are temperamentally or otherwise suited to franchising as a method of doing business. At the end of this chapter, you'll find a test designed to let you rate your readiness to franchise. But before you turn to the test, let's review some of the points to consider as you decide whether franchising is right for your business.

There is, for example, the question of autonomy. If you, as a business owner, want to retain total control over the way your business operates and how its products or services are distributed, you will not be happy as a franchisor. Although a franchisor can prescribe to a large part how a franchisee will run his unit, the franchisee does own the business, and will have the last word. That, of course, is why selection of the right franchisees is so important.

If your business is so unusual, unique, or complicated that you alone are able to operate it, then that business is not a candidate for franchising. If other normally intelligent people can't learn to operate your business effectively, they would have little or no chance to successfully "clone" your business and repeat the successes you've had.

If your business has a strictly local appeal, it is not going to lend itself well to franchising, especially on a national level. A business offering fresh orchid leis to arriving visitors might do well in Hawaii, but it would have a hard time succeeding in New York or Montana. Or if your store shows a profit because you were able to lease inexpensive retail space, it may lose money in another city where leases are more costly. If your business has limited national appeal, it may also have a reduced profit potential that would limit its franchisability. Most businesses with low sales volumes are not good candidates for franchising either, as they rarely generate revenues sufficient for the franchisor to realize any significant profits after providing the necessary support to the franchise system. (However, two workable exceptions are businesses that can be clustered or subfranchised, thereby making ownership of more than one unit standard practice, and businesses that sell only services of the owner-operator, such as Duraclean, the on-location carpet and fabric cleaning service.) Low-margin businesses are also difficult to franchise because few provide enough profit to enable the franchisees to pay royalties.

Businesses that capitalize on a hot new idea that may be forgotten six months or a year later are not franchisable. We've seen examples of franchises built around fads—pizza parlors that were highly dependent on the popularity of video games, for example—and we've seen them fail when that fad is replaced by something else.

From one unit to. . .

As we've stated, franchising is not a way to get seed capital to start a new business. You can't expect people to invest in a business concept that you haven't already tested in the marketplace. Selling franchises is second-stage financing. What you need is a proven prototype, where all of the elements of the business have been developed—a fully-functioning unit that is profitable and has been in business long enough to demonstrate its likelihood of success in the future. This prototype is an important sales tool, as we'll discuss later, and can serve to generate inquiries from potential franchisees. Even one unit can be sufficient, provided that it's doing well and the sales volume is strong.

Several of our clients have successfully entered franchising with only one unit in operation:

• Taco del Sol, a Mexican fast-food restaurant with carry-out and dining room service, began franchising in 1978. Owner Dick Drummond of Norfolk, Nebraska, operated a franchise until the parent company went out of business. He was left with a small restaurant, a lot of enthusiasm, and a good product that he felt could be successfully franchised. Dick began franchising on a shoestring, and almost lost his first franchise sale when the prospective buyer, after driving three hours from Omaha to Norfolk to see the prototype, found the old sign still up. Deep snow had prevented the sign company truck from getting close enough to the building to install the new Taco del Sol sign. Nevertheless, Taco del Sol grew steadily—if not spectacularly—and had 25 units by 1987.

• Women At Large has gotten off to a fast start in franchising by operating aerobic exercise centers for women size 16 or larger. Begun by Sharlyne Powell and Sharon McConnell, two self-described "fluffy ladies" who say they were laughed out of conventional exercise classes, Women At Large sold 10 franchises in the first year—several to women who had participated in the classes.

• David Lesser, founder of Receptions Plus, capitalized on the return to elegance and tradition in weddings. The Receptions Plus franchise provides "one-stop shopping" for photography, flowers, entertainment, formal wear, invitation printing, catering, and limousine service.

• Another client, Charles Montgomery, began franchising Beefy's Hamburgers with only three units in operation. In less than two years, 23 units were open and 19 more had been sold. Beefy's features a double drive-through window design, with a burger, soft drink, and fries selling for less than $2.00. Franchisees are attracted by the sales volumes, which are equivalent to a Wendy's in some locations, yet the initial investment is about one-eighth what it costs to become a Wendy's franchisee.

In each of the above cases, an operating prototype gave the franchisor several advantages in starting his or her franchise program: proof of the viability of the concept, experience in operations and training, and visibility to aid franchise sales. This is not to say that it's impossible to begin simultaneous development of your franchise program and your prototype. However, to do

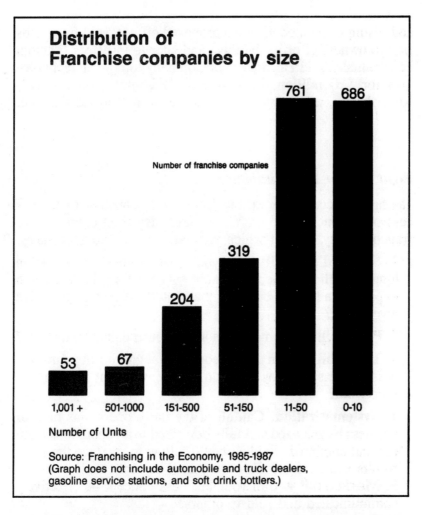

Distribution of Franchise companies by size

Number of franchise companies

Number of Units	Companies
1,001 +	53
501-1000	67
151-500	204
51-150	319
11-50	761
0-10	686

Number of Units

Source: Franchising in the Economy, 1985-1987
(Graph does not include automobile and truck dealers,
gasoline service stations, and soft drink bottlers.)

so you must have in-depth knowledge of your market and your industry, you must have the money to fund both programs, and you must have the people in place to allow you to expand in a logical manner.

One notable example of a successful franchise program that was begun without a prototype is the Headquarters Company, a business that provides office space, secretarial staffing, and even stationery on a shared basis. Michael London conceived the idea and, using small models of his proposed offices, sold franchises first to owners of office builings and later to investors. Though he eventually sold Headquarters Company to United Technologies for $20 million, he never had a company-owned unit! Nevertheless, this is indeed an exception that proves the rule.

Eight Keys to Franchisability

Taking into account the various factors that contribute to the success of a franchise program, we have identified eight keys to franchisability, against which you can measure your business:

1. Size and longevity. Has your business been in operation long enough to project its future success? Is it large enough to provide a level of earnings that would make it an attractive investment?

2. Profitability. Is it making money? Consistently? Predictably?

3. Teachability. Can other people be taught to run your business in the same way that you do, the way that has made it successful?

4. Systematization. Can all of the daily operations of your business be analyzed and fully described in an operations manual that another individual could follow to produce the same results you achieve? Can every task be replicated?

5. Marketability. Can your business concept be effectively communicated and sold to others?

6. Transferability. Can your business work just as well in another part of the country or in different market situations?

7. Originality. Do you have a point of difference from your competitors? If you're just saying, "Buy my product because I'd rather get rich than have them get rich," you are not going to be successful—in business or in franchising. Will something distinctive about your business result in consumers buying your product or service? A "hot and juicy" hamburger, for instance, or a winning marketing concept. Coastal Fitness Center, a chain of health and fitness centers for women, conducts a membership blitz before each new unit opens, thus providing the unit with start-up revenue before day-to-day expenses are incurred.

8. Affordability. A business that is profitable for you might not be profitable for the franchisee. Does enough profit remain, after a franchisee has paid the initial investment in your franchise fee, the costs of getting into business, and an ongoing royalty? Will they need significant financing? Can you help them obtain it?

TEST THE FRANCHISABILITY OF YOUR BUSINESS

Are you the next Ray Kroc? Is your business the new McDonald's? When someone asks you to describe your business, are you able to do so in a few crisp sentences? Or do you tend to ramble on about its complexities?

How about funds available to launch your franchise? Are you long on experience but short on capital? And what about your intellectual and emotional make-up? Are you more of an entrepreneur than a manager, or are you equally comfortable chasing down new ideas and making sure that the old ones are properly organized?

Now is your chance to find out. We have incorporated key factors into a simple 10-Point Franchisability Test that you can apply to your business. While not intended to replace a careful analysis of your specific business, this test should give you an idea whether—or how soon—franchising should become part of your strategy for the future. Answer these brief questions and then check the ratings to see how you measure up.

Points

1. Do you have a profitable operating prototype?
   No   1 point
   Yes   10 points   _____

2. How many units do you have in operation?
   Assign 1 point per unit up to 10.   _____

3. How long has your business been in operation?

Not in operation yet	0 points
Less than six months	2 points
One year	4 points
Two years	6 points
Three years	8 points
Four years or more	10 points

_____

4. Has anyone inquired about the possibility of buying a franchise of your business in the last year? Assign 1 point up to a total of 10 points for each inquiry by someone who is financially capable and seriously interested.

_____

5. How long would it take you to teach someone how to operate your business?

Too difficult	0 points
More than six months	5 points
Two to six months	7 points
One week to two months	10 points

_____

6. How much capital do you have available to invest in the development of a franchise program?

Under $50,000	0 points
$50,000 to $100,000	4 points
$100,000 to $150,000	6 points
$150,000 to $200,000	8 points
Over $200,000	10 points

_____

7. How many years of management experience do you have?
Assign 1 point for every year of management experience up to 10.

_____

8. How much *actual* cash would a franchisee need to open one of your units, not including the financeable portion?

$400,000 or more	2 points
$200,000 to $399,000	4 points
$100,000 to $199,000	6 points

$50,000 to $99,000	8 points	
Less than $50,000	10 points	_____

9. The market for your business or service is:

Local	2 points	
Regional	6 points	
National	8 points	
International	10 points	_____

10. Your industry is:

Highly competitive	1 point	
Moderately competitive	5 points	
Minimally competitive	10 points	_____

Total points   ☐

RATINGS

0—39: NOT READY FOR PRIME TIME. While you may have a potentially sound business concept, you have not yet conclusively demonstrated its readiness for franchising. You should concentrate upon refining the business, perhaps with the aid of professionals and experts in your industry. You may perceive that an enormous market awaits your business, but a hasty decision to franchise now could be unwise.

40—59: CLOSE, BUT QUESTIONABLE. Your business is on the borderline. It may need refinement prior to franchising. Several components are already in place, yet the likelihood for its success is in doubt—probably due to your inadequate capitalization or the need for a large investment by the franchisee.

60—79: A RISING STAR. Your chances appear quite good. You should take a very serious look at franchising as a means of expansion.

80—100: LOOK OUT, McDONALD'S! Your business has outstanding potential for rapid growth through franchising. If your assessment is correct, you have a sound concept, a broad market, and sufficient capital to make it happen. Go for it!

Franchising's Big Winners

Franchising has more than its share of success stories, a fact that's hardly surprising given its inherent fail-safe characteristics. Franchising is a system that is built for success. Witness the phenomenally low annual failure rate for franchisees of less than five percent (according to Department of Commerce figures). For new franchises, however, success is not automatic. Three requirements are: a distinctive product or service, a successful track record, and the ability to duplicate and teach your business system. And three more are determination, intelligence, and a talent for inspiring others with your own dream. Although franchising cuts across many diverse businesses, there is a common thread. Franchising is, above all, a system of doing business in which it is eminently possible to learn from the mistakes of others and to profit from their successes.

While the following capsule profiles of some of franchising's big winners are interesting and stimulating, they are included here for more than their entertainment value. Potential franchisors can benefit from more than 150 years of combined franchising experience through the examples and advice of Ray Kroc, Kemmons Wilson, Tom Monaghan, Jules Lederer, Alan Hald, and Anthony Yniguez. The stories of these franchising veterans cover, among other topics, possible pitfalls, important points in choosing franchisees, and successful formulas for planning. By following the lead of such established and successful franchises as McDonald's, Holiday Inns, Domino's Pizza, and Budget Rent A Car, franchisors can avoid some of the more common mistakes and maximize returns. All of these people achieved extraordinary success through franchising—but all of them also made significant contributions to franchising.

THE HENRY FORD OF HAMBURGERS
Ray Kroc, McDonald's

Building his fortune and fame on mass-produced meals of hamburgers, fries, and milk shakes, Ray Kroc became the most famous figure in franchising, and, indeed, in the entire food-service industry. From the day he opened his first unit in 1955, Kroc's requirements for quality, service, cleanliness, and value (QSC&V, in an oft-repeated McDonald's shorthand) became the law that McDonald's restaurants lived and prospered by. By the time of his death—in 1984—he had seen his system grow from one hamburger stand to more than 8,000 restaurants worldwide.

As we pointed out in Chapter 1, Ray Kroc did not invent franchising, fast food, or McDonald's. What he did do was to refine all three, adding his touch and vision to institutions and products that were good, or even great, but not *quite* perfect. While Kroc may not have been an inventor, he was most certainly an innovator.

Kroc started searching for his niche early in life, dropping out of high school after his sophomore year and opening a music store to highlight his piano-playing skills. When World War I began, Kroc lied about his age to become an ambulance driver overseas. He was 15 years old, and served in the same ambulance company as another underage driver who would become world famous—Walt Disney. After the war, Kroc mixed his natural talents for music and selling. He sold paper cups by day, and played piano at a radio station each night. He tried his hand at selling real estate, but was left flat broke and stranded far from home when the Florida land boom of the 1920s went bust. Kroc was only 25 when he returned to Chicago and went back to work selling cups for Lily Cup Co. He spent the next decade selling cups to street vendors, to ballparks, to cafeterias, to drugstore chains— to anyone he thought could benefit (and thereby benefit him and his employer) from use of disposable cups. This often meant inventing a new reason why various customers should buy his product—such as suggesting that Walgreen drug stores include a carryout service at their already-popular lunch counters. They followed Kroc's suggestion, and ended up becoming one of his company's largest accounts when their carryout services became a great success.

In the late 1930s, Kroc became fascinated with a multiple-mixer that one of his best cup customers had developed for mixing five malts or shakes at the same time. Convinced that the same soda fountains and ice cream shops that had been buying cups from him would see the advantage of purchasing the newly dubbed Multimixer, Kroc obtained the marketing rights to the product and quit his job at Lily to go into business for himself. After enduring a supply-oriented setback during World War II, the sales of the Multimixer soared—partly because its only initial competition was single-spindle mixers. A few years later, however, industry leader Hamilton Beach introduced a multiple-spindle mixer, and regained a large portion of the sales Kroc's company had taken away. Rather than battle his competitors directly, Kroc set out to change the market—to educate food retailers to *need* the Multimixer. This strategy worked marginally at best, but in 1954 it enabled Kroc to make a discovery that would change his life and the eating habits of the nation.

Kroc became curious as to why a California drive-in owned and run by two brothers needed 10 of his five-spindle Multimixers. He thought if he could find the answer, he could revive his company's lagging sales. Visiting the McDonald brothers' hamburger stand in San Bernardino, Kroc realized that the efficient, minimal-menu, low-cost approach the brothers employed was nearly perfect and could be easily replicated. Although he originally envisioned helping the brothers franchise their restaurant so he could sell each new McDonald's two or three Multimixers, he came to realize that the real payoff could be found in the restaurants themselves.

In 1955, Kroc opened his first McDonald's in Des Plaines, Illinois, using it from the beginning as a showcase for potential franchisees. Two years later, there were 37 McDonald's hamburger stands (indoor seating would not be introduced to the chain on a large scale until 1968), which were mostly located in the disparate climes of Southern California and the Chicago suburban area. In another two years—in 1959—the chain had reached the 100-unit mark. Kroc, of course, was the major force behind the early steady success of the chain. He had meticulously recreated—and refined and expanded—the system he had discovered in the brothers' restaurant, and had begun spreading it across the country. While extensive amounts of time, effort, and money were devoted to perfecting and promoting the franchises, the parent company, McDonald's System, Inc. (later renamed McDonald's Corporation), scraped by, and Kroc drew no salary from his new creation, instead living off a remaining trickle of Multimixer sales.

By 1961, the chain had grown to 228 units. That year, Kroc bought out the McDonald brothers' share of the company—including use of their name—for $2.7 million. This freed up the company to head unfettered in any direction that Kroc wished. That direction, spectacularly, was nowhere but up. 1969 saw the opening of the 1,000th McDonald's—three years later the total was 2,000. During this period—when McDonald's established itself as, then and since, the undisputed fast-food leader—Kroc gave much of the day-to-day control of the corporation to his trusted protege, Fred Turner. Although Kroc kept his hand in, making suggestions ranging from menu items (never his forte—his most notable failures were the meatless pineapple-and-cheese Hulaburger and miniature pound cake dessert loaves) to franchisee renewals, he allowed Turner room to operate. Growth continued at a steady upward pace—McDonald's unit total was more than 5,000 by 1980.

Although Kroc's activities with McDonald's tapered off in the early 1980s, he gained further fame and publicity when he purchased the San Diego Padres baseball team. Holding the title of senior chairman and founder, Kroc continued working full-time for McDonald's until complications from two strokes landed him in the hospital for the months before his death in 1984.

Kroc's basic philosophy called for high QSC&V standards. He understood that a franchise system cannot be completely successful until its franchisees achieve consistent levels of success. That was why the major focus in the early years was on the individual stores, rather than the corporate structure. And, while Kroc could not "teach" soda fountain owners to need Multimixers, he wrought revolutionary changes in the food supply and processing industries—even impacting the raising of cattle and the growing of potatoes—through the market strength of McDonald's huge needs.

GIVING THE PUBLIC WHAT IT WANTS
Kemmons Wilson, Holiday Inns

Before Kemmons Wilson debuted his Holiday Inns in the early 1950s, motels were generally shabby wayside stopovers for salesmen and other various transients. By introducing classy amenities—such as swimming pools, televisions, and telephones—and dependable service to motels, while maintaining a low price, Wilson's inns became homes-away-from-home for millions of American travelers. Holiday Inns were able to establish their dominance because Wilson filled what he accurately perceived to be a need in the marketplace.

In the summer of 1951, Kemmons Wilson took his family on an unpleasant vacation that proved to be the root of his eventual—and phenomenal—success. Driving from Memphis to Washington, D.C., with his wife and five children in the family station wagon, Wilson was infuriated to discover a succession of unclean, uncomfortable, over-priced motels. The final insult to Wilson was having to pay extra for each of the children, even though they were sharing their parents' room and sleeping on bedrolls they carried from home. Wilson returned to Memphis, vowing to build a motel that would eliminate the shortcomings he had experienced. The next year, Wilson's first Holiday Inn opened for business.

Since childhood, Wilson's life has been marked by a strong aptitude for business and a drive for success. His father died when Wilson was nine months old, leaving his mother to support herself and her only child. When his mother lost her job during the Depression, Wilson quit high school to get a job. Wanting to go into business for himself, Wilson bought a $50 popcorn machine for generous terms—nothing down and a dollar a week. After striking a deal with a local movie theater manager to rent space and electricity, Wilson installed the machine in the theater's lobby, and began selling popcorn. The now-common practice of selling popcorn at the movies was a new idea in Memphis at the time, and Wilson did terrific business. Before long he was making $30 a week—nearly 10 times the cost of his rent and the payments on the machine. Soon after that, Wilson was making more than the theater's manager, who promptly took over the concession, and bought the popper from Wilson for the same amount—$50—he had paid for it less than a year before. (Years later, Wilson bought the popper back again, and displayed it in his office as a sort of trophy of his first business success.) Wilson used the $50 to buy five second-hand pinball machines, which he parlayed into a route of pinball machines, cigarette machines, and jukeboxes. By 1933, two years after parting with the popper, Wilson had literally saved enough nickels—from his machines—to build a house. Once the house was finished, and Wilson discovered he could borrow against it to further finance new businesses, he never looked back.

His next ventures included a jukebox distributorship, a local chain of movie theaters, and an airplane—he gave dollar rides in it while his future wife sold tickets and his mother sold popcorn to the crowd of onlookers. But, Wilson realized, after the experience with his home (and the subsequent financing he was able to receive), that the real opportunities for growth were in the building business.

When the U.S. entered World War II, Wilson sold all of his property (realizing $250,000, which he invested in war bonds), and joined the Air Transport Command. After spending two years flying a hazardous route over the Himalayas, Wilson returned to Memphis in 1945. He acquired an Orange Crush distributorship, but lost $100,000 on it. He then followed his instinct back to construction, and began making his fortune on the post-war building boom. By the time Wilson and his family took their fateful vacation in 1951, he was worth more than $1 million, including a growing empire of homes, apartment buildings, and movie theaters.

Wilson returned to Memphis after his disappointing vacation with both the determination and the means to build a better hotel. He ordered plans for a large motel—120 rooms, as opposed to the then-usual 20-25 rooms. The draftsman who drew up the plans captioned them "Holiday Inn," after the 1942 Bing Crosby movie of the same name. Wilson liked the name, and in 1952 opened the first Holiday Inn on one of the main approach roads to Memphis.

"I put into Holiday Inns the things I liked," Wilson says. "I wanted to include what we had missed in those other motels." Swimming pools, free parking, televisions and telephones in every room, ice and soft drink machines, no extra charge for children—these features have become commonplace in motels, but Holiday Inns introduced many of them, and was the first chain of motels to offer them all.

A year-and-a-half after the first Inn opened, three more were built on other roads heading into Wilson's hometown. "You just had to go by a Holiday Inn to get into Memphis," he says. Wilson began dreaming of a national chain of hotels. In fact, he whimsically traces his initial push into franchising to a promise he made his wife. "I made a bold statement to my wife after I opened the first four Inns," Wilson recalls. "I told her that I would soon have *400* Holiday Inns across the country. Well, I realized that was quite a large number of motels. That's when I decided to look into franchising as a means of expansion." Wilson's next step was contacting "the biggest-thinking man" he knew—Wallace Johnson, a fellow Memphian with considerable contacts in the construction business. Together they formed Holiday Inns of America (now Holiday Inns, Inc.), and began franchising the motels. In their first major push, they invited 75 of the country's leading homebuilders to Memphis to pitch the Holiday Inn concept to them. About 60 of the builders showed up, and nearly all of them reacted enthusiastically when they heard the franchising proposal. Wilson envisioned a speedy start toward the realization of his grand dream. "We figured the builders would all rush home and start work on their Holiday Inns," he recalls. "We pictured all these Inns springing up practically overnight." However, within the next year, only three of these builders had begun erecting Holiday Inns. "We realized we would have to do it ourselves if we wanted the program to go anywhere," Wilson says.

Wilson and Johnson experienced more success with the next groups they approached. Appealing to doctors, lawyers, and other professionals, they began selling franchises. "We went after people with money, and put them together with people who knew how to build," Wilson recalls. By 1957, 50 Holiday Inns had opened, and the franchise got a tremendous boost as the interstate highway system began crisscrossing the country and inviting vacationers to the road. In this period, Holiday Inns developed its most visible symbol, a classic piece of roadside pop-culture known as the "Great Sign." The colorful starburst, flowing neon script, and flashing arrow pointed many a traveler to the front desk of a Holiday Inn. (Although the "Great Sign" is still extant at many Holiday Inns, it is being phased out in favor of a more sedate sign.)

In 1959, the 100th Holiday Inn was opened. Franchisees were no longer scarce—the company began thoroughly screening applicants for business and financial references. By 1965, when the Holidex computerized reservation system was introduced, the chain had mushroomed to more than 500 units. Four years later, the total was more than 1,000, and the *Sunday Times* of London included Wilson on its list of the 1,000 most important men of the 20th Century.

The early 1970s were a trying time for Holiday Inns. Although total units surpassed 1,500 by 1973, competitors—such as Ramada Inns, Howard Johnson's, and Quality Inns—were chopping steadily away at the lead Holiday Inns had built. The early 1970s also saw largely unsuccessful attempts at diversification of the parent company. Acquisitions included a faltering bus line, a meatpacking company, a campground chain, a catering service, a dinette manufacturer, and other disparate businesses. But the most crippling blow to the company came during the 1973 oil crisis. The lack of fuel kept many motorists off the roads, and the ensuing recession kept droves more from vacationing. Holiday Inns profits and stock price plummetted, and new growth slowed to a crawl. The next five years saw gradual stabilization of the company, which jettisoned some of its more incongruous acquisitions. But the days of seemingly limitless growth were long past, and what had started as a result of a particularly keen personal vision had become a tangled, multi-billion-dollar company.

After suffering a heart attack in 1979, Wilson retired as Holiday Inn, Inc.'s chairman, but soon found that a life of leisure wasn't his style. "Retirement is not for me," he said. "I need to keep busy." Wilson kept busy afterward with his Wilson World hotel (which he envisions as the first hotel in a possible mini-chain) and his Orange Lake Country Club, both located in Orlando, Florida.

Looking back, Wilson believes the credit for the success of Holiday Inns must be shared with the hundreds of franchisees who shared at least part of his dream over the years. "It worked because we had the right people out there working for us *and* for themselves. People work harder when they're working for themselves. I think that's the only way to get the most and the best out of people."

MANAGING THROUGH ADVERSITY
Tom Monaghan, Domino's Pizza

In 25 years, Domino's Pizza has grown from a handful of college-campus pizza restaurants to a world-wide chain with nearly 4,000 outlets. But before Domino's became so phenomenally successful, it encountered a number of critical obstacles that threatened the company's existence. Tom Monaghan's management skills—including a top-to-bottom devotion to details that is found today in his employees—helped his company overcome these setbacks, and made Domino's one of the fastest-growing food franchises in the U.S.

It's a long road from being a resident of the St. Joseph's Home for Boys in Jackson, Michigan, to heading one of the largest and fastest-growing fast-food franchises in the U.S. The years that saw Tom Monaghan journey from childhood in an orphanage to fame and fortune through Domino's Pizza were filled with enough drama and setbacks for any number of soap operas. But throughout those years, Monaghan's desire to succeed and his iron-willed determination remained unflagging. Once an eight-year-old who listened to Detroit Tigers games on radio, Monaghan now owns his favorite baseball team; once a 23-year-old who delivered pizzas to college students, he now owns the country's second-largest pizza chain, and claims credit for half the pizzas delivered in the U.S. each year.

Monaghan's sometimes-Dickensian journey began when he was four years old, when his father died on Christmas Eve. Unable to support the family on her own, Monaghan's mother placed him and his brother in a series of orphanages and foster homes.

(Monaghan even spent a short time in a juvenile detention center.) By the time he was 14, Monaghan was supporting himself on a work farm, but he was mischievous, and found it difficult to apply himself in school. One of his childhood dreams had been to become a priest, and he entered a seminary in his mid-teens, only to be expelled a year later, for refusing to follow the strict rules. After struggling through his remaining high school years, Monaghan wanted to go to college, but lacked both the money and the self-discipline for higher learning. He instead enlisted in the Marines, and spent a three-year stint overseas. It was during his spare time in the Marines that Monaghan discovered various self-help books, of which he remains a devoted reader and advocate. He returned to Michigan with a renewed body, mind, and spirit, as well as the determination to study architecture in college.

To raise money for school, Monaghan and his brother, Jim, obtained a small loan in 1960 to buy a pizzeria in Ypsilanti, Michigan, near the campus of Eastern Michigan University. The next year, Tom Monaghan swapped a Volkswagen for Jim's share of the restaurant, and a fledgling pizza empire was born.

Over the next three years, Monaghan began modifying his first pizza restaurants into the streamlined operations that would become Domino's. Sit-down dining was eliminated and non-pizza menu items were dropped, so the restaurants—numbering three at this stage, all near college campuses—could concentrate on speedy preparation and delivery of pizza. Monaghan's goal was to deliver all orders within 30 minutes of placement, and he guaranteed this delivery time by offering a discount if the pizza was late. These changes—plus the selection of a new name for all three restaurants—proved popular, and Domino's Pizza began to grow.

From 1965 to 1968, Domino's had grown to eight stores through franchising, and was enjoying good sales. The next four years would see the company grow six-fold through the use of franchising, but it would also bring a series of obstacles which would nearly ruin Monaghan and Domino's. In 1968, the chain's head-quarters, all of the company's records, its commissary, and its highest-grossing store were destroyed in a fire. The property was woefully underinsured, and the settlement only covered one-tenth of the loss. Already committed to opening new stores, Mona-ghan and his staff managed to press on and opened five stores in the months following the fire. The following year, preparing to take the company public, Monaghan relied on some flawed advice, and quickly expanded both the number of stores and the number of executives overseeing these new franchises. By 1970 there were 44 Domino's outlets, but there were too many bosses and new levels of bureaucracy in the company. Taxes and loans went unpaid, royalties went uncollected, and company support of the new franchises dwindled. Monaghan was temporarily re-moved from control of the company by his creditors, and had to sit idly by as things only got worse. Although Monaghan was not legally scheduled to regain even partial control of Domino's for another two years, the bank handed the company back to its founder 10 months later, because the appointed manager had failed to turn the company around, and had further alienated franchisees. Monaghan pared the company's staff down to the bare essentials, and set the company back on the road to financial health. By running the company's office during the day and working in the stores at night—making or delivering pizzas, manning the phones or counter—he was able to help pull the company back into the black and regain the confidence of franchisees.

Domino's numbered more than 100 outlets in 1975, and faced one final hurdle before the company achieved complete success. Amstar Corp., the maker of Domino Sugar, filed a trademark infringement lawsuit against Domino's Pizza. The five-year bat-tle to retain the company's name was ultimately successful and strengthened the loyalty not only of Domino's executives, but also of the franchisees, some of whom had used the Domino's name for more than 15 years by the suit's end.

After the lawsuit, in 1980, Domino's outlets totaled nearly 400, with approximately 70 percent of these stores franchised. (The

30/70 company-owned/franchised ratio has been fairly constant throughout Domino's history.) Most of these stores served college or military towns, the chain's tried-and-true customer pools. The challenge to Monaghan and his company was to expand into urban and suburban regions, while maintaining the level of quality and efficiency that had become Domino's hallmark.

As Domino's continued to grow—with an average annual growth rate of 45 percent for each of the next six years—a large part of the company's success could be traced to its method of choosing franchisees and its treatment and training of employees. Domino's estimates that 98 percent of its franchises are owned and operated by former employees of the chain. In fact, as we have noted earlier, at least one year's experience with Domino's is the current requirement of anyone wishing to purchase a franchise. A corps of knowledgeable franchisees helps maintain top-to-bottom quality, as well as foster a sense of loyalty. And this experience is backed up with a commitment of on-going company training, support, and supervision. Each outlet is visited monthly or even semi-monthly by company consultants and field representatives. Incentives—thought of or inspired by Monaghan—are available to productive franchisees, managers, and other employees. For example, any store manager that exceeds the current company weekly sales record—now over $62,000—receives a $15,000 Swiss watch from Monaghan. (Monaghan had given away at least six such watches by the mid-1980s.)

By early 1987, Domino's had nearly 4,000 outlets, and opened an average of three new stores each day. The chain has established its presence in urban areas and is continuing to expand according to schedule. In the pizza business, only PepsiCo's Pizza Hut has more outlets, and Domino's estimates it will pass Pizza Hut around 1990, and zoom on toward its goal of 10,000 stores by the mid '90s. Foreign expansion is also a priority. There are Domino's in Canada, the United Kingdom, West Germany, Australia, and Japan. By the time Domino's hits 10,000 units it is estimated that 10 percent of those outlets will be located abroad.

This grand level of success has brought Monaghan a great deal of publicity and the ability to fulfill some of his lifelong dreams. He never got to play shortstop for his beloved Detroit Tigers (as he boasted he would back at the orphanage), but instead bought the Tigers in 1984. The team won the World Series in Monaghan's first year of ownership. He never got to study architecture in college, but he is regarded today as a knowledgeable devotee of Frank Lloyd Wright architecture and a major collector of Wright furniture. Construction is underway on Domino's Farms, a 300-acre complex of office, conference, and medical facilities in a bucolic setting outside of Ann Arbor, Michigan. Monaghan's philosophy of business mirrors his beliefs—and experiences—in life: learn all you can from your mistakes, treat others as you would have them treat you (or your pizza store), and maintain high ethical and moral standards.

Monaghan admits he has a large appetite for life and the good things it can offer him, but he does not forget the base that enabled him to create such a life. Each week he tries to set aside time to visit a few Domino's stores. He has an innate feel of when a store is running right just by its busy rhythm. He gets into that rhythm, and many times starts tossing pizza dough, twirling it on his fingers long after the publicity cameras have stopped clicking. He is, after all, the self-proclaimed "greatest pizza store manager who ever walked." He is, of course, quite pleased to be a multimillionaire, and still can't believe he owns his favorite baseball team, but he realizes from whence his fortune came. "I'm a pizza man, " Tom Monaghan says. "I'm proud of that."

LEARNING TO BE A GOOD PARENT
Jules Lederer, Budget Rent A Car

From a trial-and-error beginning in the late 1950s, Jules Lederer built Budget Rent A Car into the first nationwide discount car rental chain. Starting with no experience in either the car-rental or franchising businesses, Lederer expanded the company by relying on franchisees who were both enthusiastic about the Budget concept and financially sound.

The training and nurturing of these franchisees paid off—Budget franchises numbered more than 500 world-wide when the company was sold to Transamerica in 1968.

Jules Lederer, founder of Budget Rent A Car, admits that what he knew about franchising in 1960—when he started franchising Budget— "would fit on the head of a pin. I didn't have a clue," he said. What he did have was a solid business background in sales and marketing and the desire for a new challenge. In 1958, one of his cousins opened a rental-car office in Los Angeles with 48 used cars and a plan to undercut the prices charged by car rental's Big Two—Hertz and Avis. He invited Lederer out to California to look at his operation and asked Lederer's advice. "I told him that his name—Budget—and his concept seemed like winners, but told him he needed new cars to appeal to the largest number of people." Lederer bankrolled the company's first 100 automobiles, and dependable discount car rental—using new cars—was born.

By renting at half-price the same cars the "big boys" (as Lederer refers to Hertz and Avis) offered, Budget was able to establish its niche in the marketplace, often without competing head-to-head with the other companies. "Most of their offices were located at major airport terminals, but we weren't. We were near the airport, but also near residential and commercial areas, so we were appealing to more than just travelers," Lederer recalls.

After two profitable years, Lederer decided that Budget was ripe for growth. "I knew I didn't have the money to expand Budget through normal corporate channels," Lederer says. "I just didn't have the money to go after Hertz and Avis on my own." A friend, Kemmons Wilson, suggested that Lederer expand his company the way Wilson had expanded Holiday Inns—through franchising. A combination of economic realities and the conviction that he could sell his expertise convinced Lederer that franchising was the best way to spread Budget from coast to coast—and beyond.

"I entered the car-rental business with a wealth of ignorance and total inexperience," Lederer says. "But I think it was better that way—I had no 'sacred cows' to deal with, no carved-in-stone dos and don'ts. It seemed that sharing the knowledge we had acquired—through trial and error—with enthusiastic franchisees, who were also new to the car rental business, was the only viable way to expand Budget."

Media mentions resulted in the first two Budget franchises being sold in Chicago and Hawaii. Using Avis as a model, Lederer set up a franchise fee and royalty schedule that was based on flat amounts, and did not allow for larger percentages as each franchise grew. This cost his young company a considerable sum. Lederer views the cost of that mistake as his tuition. "Franchise consulting firms didn't exist then. In retrospect, the fee for experienced guidance would have cost me far less than those first mistakes did."

The next two years saw Budget grow quickly. By 1962, the company had 50 franchises located across the country, and a low failure rate. Lederer credits this to both extensive training and financial screening of franchisees. "It didn't make sense to take a fee and collect a royalty from someone just for the sake of having the upfront money and another office if I wasn't sure they could make a successful go of it."

This attention to detail, along with a dedication to building as a team, helped make Budget a growing alternative to the big boys. "I knew my success depended on the franchisees," says Lederer, "and they knew that their continued prosperity depended on me." In 1964, Budget had just under 100 franchises operating in the U.S. Four years later, the number had grown to more than 300, plus approximately 180 franchises located abroad. "I knew Budget could be expanded into Canada and Europe, but I also knew that it would take time and that I could not treat these markets simply as extensions of the United States. A common language does not necessarily mean common business customs."

In 1968, just eight years after Budget began franchising, the company agreed to be acquired in an exchange of stock by Transamerica Corporation, a financial and insurance company. Lederer profited handsomely from this deal, and he remained with Budget and Transamerica for another four years before an amicable parting. "I discovered that an entrepeneur does not make a good corporate soldier," he says.

Looking back, Lederer sees three key points that helped Budget succeed—points, he believes, from which any fledgling franchisor can benefit. First, there must be a valid, well-defined concept that has proven itself and that has universal appeal. (Though Budget's start was rather haphazard, he suggests market research and planning.) Second is the selection of qualified, enthusiastic, and financially-able franchisees. "If I grant a franchise to someone who is short of money, and he ends up failing because of this, not only is the company out his fees and royalty—it hurts the franchise's name and reputation." Lederer's third recommendation is to provide on-going training and support. "The relationship between the franchisor and franchisee is basically parental," Lederer says. "The franchisee places his trust—and money—with the franchisor, and in return, he must receive guidance. Both parties must be determined to make it work."

PARTNERS IN PROFIT
Alan Hald, MicroAge

In the rapidly changing world of computers, MicroAge Computer Stores have remained a reliable constant, offering the latest in computer software and hardware, as well as on-going training and support. Alan Hald, MicroAge's co-founder and chairman, credits the company's growth to its level of vision and commitment. By establishing long-term relationships with its franchisees, vendors, and customers, MicroAge is poised to continue its growth and prosperity.

In 1973, when an apple was still just a piece of fruit and IBM's major office product was still typewriters, Alan Hald had what he calls an "intuitive feeling" about the future of microelectronics. He envisioned the growth of microprocessor technology, and the diffusion of this technology throughout all levels of business. At that time, computers were generally bulky, expensive machines used only by large businesses. But the next two years saw the birth of the microcomputer industry, and the initial attempts at distributing computers and their related materials through consumer-oriented stores. It was seeing an independent store selling one of the first personal computers in 1975 that helped provide the impetus that led Hald and Jeff McKeever to leave First Interstate Bank of Arizona and found MicroAge. In 1976, MicroAge became the first computer store in Arizona, and one of only a handful of such stores in the country.

As the microcomputer industry changed in the waning years of the 1970s—moving from serving hobbyists to a broader segment of the general public—the stores that sold personal-computer hardware and software changed as well. While many sold combinations of computer hardware and software—along with computer furniture and other accessories—MicroAge was one of the first to offer complete solutions to personal and business computing needs. MicroAge sought to position itself as a store which did more than just make a sale and hand a customer an instruction book. Systems of training, support, and service were developed to accompany the equipment and materials that the store sold. In 1979, *Business Week* called this approach "a tough way to sell computers," but it turned out to be a good on-going way to attract repeat customers.

Three years after its inception, in 1979, MicroAge numbered six stores, and was the largest company-owned microcomputer chain in the U.S. At this point, an estimated six percent of all the microcomputer products sold in the country passed through MicroAge's central warehouse. The company's next expansion move, in 1980, was through franchising. "The computer industry is characterized by the rapid generation and turnover of technology and know-how," Hald says. "By franchising MicroAge, we knew we could create an 'island of stability' to retain and manage this ever-changing flow of know-how within each store. In a company-owned environment, upward movement and promotion of people can dissipate knowledge; franchising allows for expansion of resources and individuals while retaining a complete body of knowledge at a level accessible to the customer."

One year into its expansion-through-franchising program, MicroAge hit a number of stumbling blocks that could have meant ruin for a company whose management had less dedication and vision. During the recession of 1981, the company found itself unable to completely meet the upfront financial challenge of building a rapidly-growing franchise program. This financial shortfall, combined with a delay in signing central purchasing agreements with major vendors, forced MicroAge to seek the protection and reorganization of a Chapter 11 bankruptcy. Unique to the situation was the fact that MicroAge managed to continue expansion—including selling its first franchises abroad—and keep most of its key employees during reorganization. Eleven years after MicroAge's founding—and six years after the reorganization—Hald and McKeever remain two of the few microcomputer executives in the industry still with the company they started. (In 1986, both were hailed among the top 25 industry executives in *Computer Reseller News*.)

From 1981 to 1984, popularity and sales of personal and integrated business computers soared. MicroAge's committed "solutions" program was drawing an ever-growing portion of the business computer market, and the number of MicroAge franchises continued to expand. During this period, marked by a volatile business climate in which stores—and indeed, entire chains—seemed to open and close almost overnight, MicroAge enjoyed stability for a number of reasons. "Our strategy has always entailed taking ideas into action. 'Where vision becomes reality' is a company trademark, and to that end we want to establish long-term relationships with our franchisees," Hald explains. "Our franchise agreement is longer than the industry average—10 years for the first term, with options for renewal afterwards. We feel this commitment allows us a broader perspective, which has helped MicroAge adapt to changes in the marketplace."

After 1984, as supply began to exceed the still-fervent demand for computers, the number of computer specialty stores began declining. The industry view held that the market was maturing, and, after the first personal-computer boom, a period of changing needs would follow. Consumers were concerned about obsolescence, compatibility, and upgradability of the products available. Business computer users especially had a need for service and support. These factors encouraged the growth of systems-oriented stores, and positioned MicroAge as a pioneer and industry leader in this approach.

Through early 1987, MicroAge had expanded to nearly 200 locations, including franchises in Canada, West Germany, France, Italy, the United Kingdom, and Japan. More than 30 percent of the company's new stores since 1984 have come from conversions of independent computer stores—a conversion/subfranchisor arrangement has made MicroAge the second-largest computer store chain in Canada. Hald believes that independents are clearly recognizing the value of the MicroAge name—and vision—in the marketplace. "We focus on profits through partnership—partnership between the organization, the franchisees, the vendors, and the client base. We stress to the franchisees that 'your success is our success,' and we back that up with our level of support, communication, and business strategy. I believe that such a partnership—and the trust behind it—is critical for success."

Hald, a member of the World Future Society, sees an important social and economic role for franchising in the coming years. He believes that the transmittal of proven business strategies—rather than the sale of actual goods and services—will grow in importance, and he sees franchising as an established and focused conduit for the flow of such information. "Franchising looks to become even more pervasive as a business vehicle in the coming years," he says. "Franchising can influence changes in social structures throughout the world, because it effectively transfers know-how, and plants the seeds of a capitalist economy and individual freedoms. Franchising is in the process of spreading a worldwide revolution of free enterprise and free expression. When franchising is accepted in the Soviet Union and/or China, these societies will rapidly advance in freedom, growth, and achievement. I believe this can happen over the next 50 years."

Just as portions of U.S. culture have been exported throughout the world by franchising, Hald believes that the future will see Japanese and European influences being exerted on the U.S. through what he calls "reverse franchising" from overseas. "As other nations become adept at franchising a concept or business, rather than just exporting goods, we will see interesting cultural and economical changes. For example, if a Japanese company exports sushi to the U.S., money is made for the company and a need is simply served. However, if a sushi restaurant is franchised from Japan into the U.S., the product and the know-how— the particular management techniques—are exported, a flow of money back to Japan (through fees and royalties) is established, and jobs are created in the U.S." Hald sees this sort of cultural and economic exchange benefitting both countries, and setting the stage for further exchanges of know-how and capital. Hald envisions this as potentially revolutionary, and all but inevitable. "There is no doubt in my mind," he firmly states, "that the primary economic battles of the next 50 years will be waged mostly through franchise vehicles."

SPREADING THE FRANCHISING UMBRELLA
Anthony Yniguez, Red Carpet Realty

Entering a fragmented market of independent realty offices in the mid-1960s, Anthony Yniguez introduced the power of a unified name and image to real estate through franchising. By converting established real estate agents to franchisees, Red Carpet was able to take advantage of experience in the field, and build on it through advertising and skilled management. This strong base helped Red Carpet survive through a period that saw the rise and subsequent demise of many other real estate franchisors.

In 1962, at the age of 39, Anthony Yniguez had spent 15 years selling real estate and running a realty office. In that time, he had come to realize that the industry as a whole was disjointed and that many individual realty offices were poorly run. "I asked myself why one of the largest businesses in the world wasn't better organized," Yniguez says. "I wondered why some real estate firms couldn't share one image and pool their costs and risks to benefit all. I also came to realize that in the average real estate office, one-third of the people were learning the business, one-third were producing, and one-third were planning to leave."

Convinced of the potential for a unified chain, Yniguez took a year-long "retirement," and spent much of his time closely observing the real estate industry and its trends. "I tried to fully understand the business. I learned that the real estate and construction businesses together then had a dollar volume second only to the combined expenditures for food and tobacco. It seemed to me that the volume was much too high not to benefit a large entity," Yniguez recalls. His attorney agreed, advising Yniguez to go national before somebody else did. In 1966, after three years of planning, development, and experimentation, Red Carpet Corporation of America was born, and five Red Carpet Realty offices opened in California's Contra Costa County.

"I wasn't thinking about growth when I began franchising Red Carpet, although it is important," Yniguez admits. "My main concern was the ability to provide service to the public. With individual realty offices, everyone was concerned with establishing a local image, and spending money on maintaining that image. To me, it seemed obvious that by creating a unified image for a number of offices, we could save time and money and offer better service to the public. I thought that if this was done correctly and professionally, growth would logically follow." Another logical step in the growth of Red Carpet was to convert already successful, independent real estate offices to franchises. (Other Red Carpet franchises were opened by experienced real estate people who broke away from independent offices—none of the offices were company-owned units.) "The selection of the right franchisees was very important," Yniguez recalls. "We only approached 30 percent of the brokers in any given area about becoming Red Carpet franchisees. Local success was a factor in selection, but sometimes potential was even more important. We took on a number of very small offices that became quite large." As in any conversion-oriented franchising program, Red Carpet encountered resistance to change. "In asking a broker to replace his name with Red Carpet's name, we often ran into ego problems. But, in most cases, the strength of our unified image and our commitment to support won out."

Another strong selling point in Red Carpet's favor was the power of advertising. In an era when the only form of advertising most realty offices relied on was the sign outside their doors, Red Carpet was able to afford mass advertising, including television and newspaper ads, billboards, and mailings. "Our advertising multiplied the strength of the company's name. As we grew in publicity, larger numbers of independents would agree to join the system. We were then able to enlarge the scope of the advertising, attract more clients and more franchises, and so on. This business, like many others, is a constant game of numbers—the bigger numbers, the better." Red Carpet's ability to pool funds for local and national advertising exposure was a strong selling point. "When I could tell brokers that I could take the $1,000 they were using to promote themselves locally and literally multiply it by 100, they would just run for their pocketbooks. That was the power of the unified name."

Quickly spreading from northern California to the rest of the state, then to Arizona and Oregon, Red Carpet had more than 100 franchises in 1971 after five years of operation. Two years later, the number had climbed to more than 500, and included new franchises in Texas, Florida, and Connecticut. The next few years of the mid-1970s would see other franchise companies of varying size enter the real estate business. While many of these fledgling chains offered only advertising support or partial training to their franchisees, Century 21, the most successful of these new franchises, followed the Red Carpet method of providing full service, from training and support down to referrals and colorful company blazers. (In a 1978 *Washington Star* article, Century 21 founder Art Bartlett admitted copying everything he could from Red Carpet, a fact Yniguez proudly points out.)

Despite these competitors and a sluggish economy, Red Carpet continued growing, reaching 700 franchises in 1976 and its peak of more than 1,200 franchises in 30 states in 1979. "When I left the day-to-day management of Red Carpet in 1979, there were more than 45 franchised companies selling real estate across the country," Yniguez recalls. "Inflation, recession, and high interest rates shook up the realty business in the next few years. By 1983, partially because of the economy and partially by attrition—some of our brokers had been running offices for 15 years by then and many were retiring—the number of Red Carpet franchises stabilized at more than 800 in 28 or 29 states. The 45 other real estate franchisors that were competing with us in 1979 had declined to less than 10 of any decent size in that same four-year period." In 1983, 21 years after his "early retirement," Yniguez sold Red Carpet, which was acquired the next year by a San Diego-based mortgage company.

In general, Yniguez feels that successful franchising must begin with a plan that has been proven viable. "A good idea does not necessarily make for a good business. An idea needs proven methods and an identifiable image." He also cites financial planning, a realistic growth plan, and communication with franchisees as being important. "I would strongly advise a franchisor to listen to franchisees—pay attention to the people who have constant contact with your public. Ask these people what would make this franchise—and the entire system—more successful. And then listen to their answers." A corollary to this point, Yniguez adds, is maintaining quality people at all levels of operation. "We looked for good people—from eager young men and women with little experience to managers successfully running half-a-dozen offices—and then trained them well. And it really paid off."

Yniguez sees the future of real estate as belonging to the brokers that are associated with a powerful franchise. "By and large, the most successful entities in the real estate business today are franchised. Franchises are exceptionally strong and have the funds to take advantage of technological advances, both in training agents and serving clients. This concept is very important to the real estate industry." Or, in the words of French writer Victor Hugo—words Yniguez adopted as a personal and (unofficial) corporate motto— "No army can withstand the strength of an idea whose time has come."

Up and Comers

"What a clever idea!" How often is this phrase repeated around the country when some new franchise begins popping up like daffodils after a spring shower? Of course, that's only a part of the story. Clever ideas are a dime a dozen within the world of retail business. Most of them never make it. Among those that *do* make it are often the ideas that get franchised. And therein lies the crucial difference between a clever idea and an idea that is both clever *and* successful.

Franchising, really, is a way of replicating success. And, because many successful ideas are in some way innovative, there's always room for a new kid on the block. A franchise might be built on a new twist to an existing idea. For example, department stores and some furniture outlets traditionally have carried a small selection of juvenile furniture, but The Baby's Room changed the rules of that market by offering a comprehensive selection in one location at lower prices. Or a franchise may be launched off a brand-new concept, such as the notion of capturing a large chunk of the multi-million-dollar indoor-plant market, as Silk Plants, Etc. has done by retailing authentic-looking decorator silk plants that require little care or upkeep.

Our company, Francorp, Inc., helps many businesses who view franchising as an exciting opportunity. We provide an efficient formula for replicating their successful and innovative business systems in new markets. The following short profiles of "Up and Comers"—businesses that have the potential to become mega-franchises—are but a small cross-sampling of new and interesting franchise organizations drawn from the list of Francorp's present and former clients. These do not necessarily represent the fastest growing or most profitable franchisors in the field today. But they do, we believe, offer to franchise watchers—and to anyone about to test the waters—a feel for the kinds of ventures that could make it big in franchising.

SHEAR GENIUS
Hair Performers

John Amico's pioneering efforts in beauty and hair-care began in 1960, when he opened his first salon. During the next decade, Amico opened a cosmetology school and a successful salon in a large suburban Chicago shopping mall. Wanting to move away from what he calls the "traditional beauty shop and barber shop image—offering assembly-line haircuts at rock-bottom prices," Amico opened his first Hair Performers salons in 1972.

Hair Performers franchises were first offered in 1977, but after signing up only two franchisees in the first six months, Amico came to recognize the differences between the franchising business and the hair-care business. "You might be terrific in the hair business, but that doesn't mean that you will have a successful franchise. I learned that franchising is a business in and of itself, and requires specific expertise."

Amico spent the next two years studying franchising and perfecting Hair Performers' approach to it, rapidly increasing the number of franchise units to 50. "I came to realize the important differences between a good franchise and a bad franchise," Amico says. "A good franchise studies the inherent problems in its chosen product or service and implements a system that correctly solves these problems. A bad franchise ignores the problems and tries to apply a generic business approach to the hair-care—or whatever—industry. By franchising something we knew quite a bit about, we were able to avoid that and maintain our desired level of quality."

Hair Performers continued to grow, reaching the 100-franchise mark in 1980, then doubling to 200 in the next two years. By early 1987, 360 Hair Performers franchises had been sold in 18 states, with another unit in Taiwan. "We may not be as aggressive as some franchisors," Amico admits, "because we are more concerned about level of operations, local support, and gross volume per unit. The number of stores is not the most important thing to us—the gross per unit is." Hair Performers is able to add to the gross of each store by distributing most major professional beauty care lines, including its own. Not only does this sale of continuity products create a whole new profit center in each store, but it adds to the salon's appeal for customers. "We offer our customers a full shopping experience for beauty and hair care products," Amico says. "By offering these different brands we can establish customer loyalty and increase sales." Recently, Amico has begun a new franchise: We Care Hair, a value-priced hair salon. Begun in May 1986, We Care Hair had 25 franchises sold just one year later.

Amico sees three points to successful franchising in general. The first is offering a great product or service. "I don't mean an average product or even a good one," he says. "You must be able to compete with your industry's best. You must be on the highest level of competition." Second is consistent delivery of this product or service. "No matter where a customer finds a Hair Performers—in Chicago or Phoenix—they are assured of the same level of service." Amico's final point concerns training of employees. "You must be able to replicate your concept in a simple manner so average people can do superior jobs," he says.

Amico believes strongly that the franchisor's success depends completely on franchisees. "The franchisees must be successful before the franchisor can ever be," Amico says. "A viable business must stand the test of time on all levels. To succeed, a franchisor must provide excellent service to both franchisees and day-to-day customers." To help develop this success, Amico has kept Hair Performers responsive and supportive as the scope of operations has grown. "I first thought I was in the hair business," he recalls. "Then I thought that I was in the people development business. Then I thought I was in the communication business. And now, after all that, I finally realize that as franchisors, we are ultimately in the business of education."

MAJOR LEAGUE IDEA
Merle Harmon's Fan Fair

The true sports fan wears his team's colors with pride—it's a symbol of loyalty. That's what Merle Harmon counts on for the growth of his Fan Fair stores. But the Fan Fair customer not only can wear his team logo, he can drink out of it, sit on it, hang it on a wall, or use it to decorate his Christmas tree. Fan Fair stores can imprint the name or logo of almost every professional or college team onto almost any gift or novelty item.

Merle Harmon should know about sports fans. He has been a broadcaster for the Milwaukee Braves (before they moved to Atlanta), the Milwaukee Brewers, and the Texas Rangers baseball teams. With the popularity of nationally televised sports, and the increased mobility of the population, a sports team's fans are often scattered throughout the country. And college sports fans, of course, often settle far from their alma maters. While in Milwaukee, Harmon noticed that, although hometown souvenirs were everywhere, it was difficult to find a gift with the emblem of an out-of-town team or an out-of-state college. He opened his first Fan Fair store in 1977 in the Milwaukee area to fill that need.

Once Harmon settled on a winning combination of products in his flagship outlet, he decided to open additional locations to increase market presence and profit from quantity discounts on merchandise. Three more company-owned Merle Harmon's Fan Fair stores were added by 1981.

The decision to franchise came about as a way to grow quickly while keeping the business solid. "It's like a house," Harmon says. "The foundation must be solid before the second story can be added. We're always strengthening the foundations as we grow." As the country has become increasingly sports-minded, Harmon and his franchises have found a growing number of markets. Fan Fair franchises have naturally found acceptance in major-league cities, but smaller cities, with a large number of major league and collegiate sports fans, will also support Fan Fair outlets.

Fan Fair's growth hasn't been without obstacles. It has occasionally been difficult for Fan Fair's suppliers to keep up with demand for sports-oriented products, because there may be only one vendor licensed to produce a given product. If the vendor falls behind demand, there is often nowhere else to turn for merchandise. Demand itself can be unpredictable. The fortunes of a product line can swing with the fortunes of the sports team whose emblem adorns the products. On the positive side, Fan Fair's concept has yet to attract any formidable competition. With Fan Fair's strong presence in many markets and lucrative contracts with suppliers, competition has a hard time getting started.

Since Fan Fair began franchising in 1982, 100 stores have opened in 24 states—with contracts signed for an additional 80 or more. Harmon attributes the success of Fan Fair's franchise program to a commitment to recognize the needs of franchisees. Harmon and his management team treat franchisees as customers who must be satisfied if they are going to remain loyal. Harmon knows Fan Fair can't be successful without its franchisees, and he watches their performance carefully. He plainly states his philosophy: "If my franchisee loses money, it worries the heck out of me." So far his worries have been small: All of Fan Fair's franchised and corporate stores have been successful.

Fan Fair's growth plans are conservative. Harmon hopes the long-term is what investors are looking for; not "get-rich-quick" or "pie-in-the-sky" promises, but a solid plan with the full support of the corporate organization.

According to a 1983 poll conducted by the Miller Brewing Company, 89 percent of the U.S. population are enthusiastic sports fans. With this large base to draw from, the "Sports Fan's Gift Shop" (as Fan Fair outlets are subtitled) should continue its strong growth.

DUPLICATING SUCCESS
Copy Mat

The same complaints can be heard over and over again in copy shops nationwide: "The copier broke down again;" "The copies came out fuzzy;" "I don't have enough change to make all the copies I need." Terry Fairbanks and Jim Hill must have heard these complaints often enough while working for Xerox Corporation, supplying copy-shop clients with equipment. They thought they could improve the copy industry's image and opened their own copy shop in San Francisco in 1973. Copy Mat immediately set itself apart from competitors that most often were confined to cramped quarters and restricted to bare-bones service. The Copy Mat store is large and well-designed, with a wide variety of copying options available, from self-service to overnight copying for large jobs. The store cultivated a professional image through a willingness to customize services to meet the needs of individuals or business clients. Long hours and a selection of office supplies complemented the full-service approach.

Before Copy Mat, the copy-shop business consisted mostly of offshoots of existing printing companies. Because copying was only a sideline for these companies, they did not invest heavily in equipment or in trained personnel. The result was often poor service and slipshod work which gave most copy shops a bad name. As the first full-service copy shop, Copy Mat's reputation spread quickly throughout the Bay area. Customers were pleased to find a copy shop that was clean, professional, and convenient, where the customer's needs came first. Volume increased so quickly at the first Copy Mat that another store was opened within a year.

At this point, Fairbanks and Hill were dissatisfied with the rate of growth that Copy Mat was achieving from internally-generated funds. They decided to turn to franchising as a method of growth that did not require significant company capital. Rapid growth through franchising offered a way for Copy Mat to enter new markets quickly, pre-empting would-be imitators.

The overall reputation of copy shops was an obstacle. Shopping mall owners had to be convinced that Copy Mat was not set up solely for a quick profit, but was a quality business, worthy of leasing prime space in any given mall or shopping center. Through tours of existing stores and sketches and models of planned outlets, Copy Mat was able to prove that an upscale copy-shop concept has broad appeal, and would be an asset to any shopping center.

Finding franchisees has not been difficult. Between 1984, when franchising of the stores began, and 1986, Copy Mat grew to a total of 46 stores, all but two of them franchised. Copy Mat has built a reputation for service and support of its franchisees, attracting many people—often from corporate middle management—who were dissatisfied with their career growth. Copy Mat trains its franchisees to know the market and offers discounts on equipment through volume purchases from suppliers. Franchisees are able to attract and retain qualified employees by following Copy Mat's compensation system. Employees are paid incentives for craftsmanship and correctness of work, giving them a real stake in maintaining the quality image of Copy Mat.

Fairbanks realizes that while selling copies is different from selling hamburgers, selling the franchise for either is rather similar. Copy Mat did not invent the photocopy, just as McDonald's did not invent the hamburger, but both have succeeded by providing a service that fills a niche in the marketplace. Copy Mat may never be able to claim, "Billions and billions served," as McDonald's does, but it has quickly established itself as the leader of the fledgling full-service copy-shop market.

BOOMING BUSINESS
The Baby's Room

It is apparent that the baby boomlet has arrived. The children of the original baby boom, now in their twenties and thirties, are responsible for a steady growth in America's birthrate, leading to a new demand for everything the newborn will need in the first few years. The Baby's Room is capitalizing on this baby boomlet by stocking its stores with a comprehensive selection of baby and juvenile furniture, as well as selections of baby toys and clothing.

After only 12 years of operation, The Baby's Room is the leading chain of stores in the juvenile-furniture market, outperforming some stores that have been around since the original baby boom began. Co-founder Alan Levine had experience selling baby furniture door-to-door, but no experience in retailing, when he and a partner, Vincent Powell, opened the first The Baby's Room store in suburban Chicago in 1975. They slashed the retail prices of their merchandise and advertised heavily to introduce the store. Success was immediate and took local competitors by surprise. The Baby's Room expanded quickly to six Chicago-area stores and one each in Dallas and Buffalo. Levine and Powell saw problems with this rapid expansion. The logistics of a small store chain suddenly going nationwide were an obstacle, as was attracting and training the right personnel. Above all, the expense of rapid growth was taxing the company's finances.

As a way of testing the potential market for their ideas, Levine and Powell entered into management consulting arrangements for two years, supplying seven independent furniture retailers with expertise and advice. The experiment was a success—one store increased volume 100 percent, and another, starting from scratch, with set-up and advertising advice from Levine and Powell, reached $1 million in sales in its first year. But Levine and Powell realized that, through their consulting arrangement, they were practically giving away their business system to competitors. They decided to use their knowledge to expand The Baby's Room through franchising, establishing both a market presence and a stream of continuing income—two important factors lacking in their consulting work.

In a little over a year after completing its franchise program, The Baby's Room had grown to 11 outlets, and many independent retailers of juvenile furniture had inquired about converting their outlets into The Baby's Room franchises. They were attracted by the prospect of strong advertising support and the economies of bulk purchasing. In fact, Levine estimates that franchisees' savings due to increased buying power amount to at least two percent of their gross sales—thereby offsetting about ⅔ of the three percent royalty they pay.

The Baby's Room offers specialized services to its franchisees, including purchasing, finance, training, and advertising. An innovative direct-mail marketing program targets advertising flyers to expectant parents, whose names are obtained from a variety of sources. This provides a strong customer base to help new franchisees get started and a constant source of new leads for existing franchisees. Success of the franchisees is the main priority of The Baby's Room, and a great deal of time is invested by the corporate management team in guiding and assisting franchisees.

Creating success in a franchise program is not a one-way street, however, as Levine and Powell soon learned. Their franchisees began to contribute to the chain's competitiveness very early in the game. One of the franchisees, for example, became intrigued by freight rates and routing, and learned so much about this complex field that he enabled the entire chain to negotiate lower freight costs on merchandise shipments from factories. Franchisees have also gotten deeply involved in buying decisions. Product line selections, formerly dictated by headquarters, are now made jointly at franchisee meetings, to which franchisees bring new products which they have tested locally. Alan Levine reports that after years of making such decisions himself, it was hard to get used to giving up part of his authority—but the bottom line benefit has been a great convincer!

Such creative problem-solving has strengthened the chain's marketing muscle. In the Chicago area, the success of The Baby's Room stores directly contributed to the decision by two local department stores to discontinue their lines of juvenile furniture. According to Levine, the fiercest competition comes not from other stores, however, but from hand-me-downs passed on by relatives and friends of new parents. To counteract this, The Baby's Room's sales force is trained to know about the latest safety requirements for juvenile furniture, which older products often cannot meet. New parents may then decide to purchase all new furniture to ensure the safest possible environment for their child.

Alan Levine is not shy about stating his ambitions for The Baby's Room. By catering to a growing number of affluent, two-career couples—who are willing to buy the best for their child—

Levine has stated that he expects The Baby's Room to become "the Toys 'R' Us of baby furniture."

A GROWING CONCERN
Silk Plants, Etc.

Plants are a high-demand, attractive decorating accessory. The downside is that they require a lot of care—watering, feeding, and pruning—and *still* often end up brown and wilted on the windowsill. Silk Plants, Etc. is out to prove that well-crafted silk flowers can be even better than the real thing. And if the recent phenomenal growth of this up-and-coming franchise is any indication, this premise may be right.

Silk Plants, Etc. can replace almost any plant with an amazingly life-like imitation that will never wither. The merchandise selection also includes bridal bouquets, eight-foot-tall trees, floral arrangements, and the brass, ceramic, and wicker pots to put them in.

Even though Mark Dalen had worked with plastic, silk, and dried flowers for almost 10 years, he was under 30 when he opened his first Silk Plants, Etc. store. As a sole entrepreneur, he developed his own reliable sources of imported materials and finished goods. The company prospered quickly, adding several new locations within its first few years. In 1985, Dalen, responding to requests from people who admired his stores, chose franchising as his principal expansion method. And, indeed, he sold franchises rapidly as soon as his franchise development program was completed. But as Silk Plants, Etc. grew to upward of 100 stores, Dalen was confronted with a paradox. To feed his mushrooming chain, he needed large quantities of inventory; to get this inventory, a credit line of literally millions of dollars was required. But Dalen, despite the growth of his company, was unable to obtain that kind of credit. At the same time, he also began to feel the pressures of heavier management concerns than he had ever encountered before. Into the picture stepped a large public company—Ozite Corporation—which offered an amount in excess of $5 million for Silk Plants, Etc. It was an offer Dalen could not refuse, and today he continues as Executive Vice President of Silk Plants, Etc., but also spends time watching his investments.

Franchising of Silk Plants, Etc. has proceeded quickly since 1985—by mid-1987, nearly one-third of the more than 150 Silk Plants, Etc. stores were franchises. Long-range growth plans project 800 stores nationwide by 1992, with the majority of them franchised.

Silk Plants, Etc. can predict such amazing growth because its largest potential markets are, as yet, untapped. The commercial market for artificial plants is only now beginning to be explored. In the opinion of George Burns, Vice President of Franchising for Silk Plants, Etc., many hotels, restaurants, and office buildings that currently hire plant-care services will be interested in the one-time expense of acquiring artificial plants, which require very little maintenance. Silk Plants, Etc. officials see few obstacles in reaching their optimistic goals, since they have virtually no competition. Only two other companies are currently operating franchises in the silk-flower business, but they have fewer than 20 stores combined.

Silk Plants, Etc. franchisees are typically middle managers from large organizations, whose entrepreneurial spirit has been stifled and who want a unique business opportunity. Silk Plants, Etc. offers high levels of support for its franchisees, ranging from site selection and management training to advertising assistance and continued consultation. Silk Plants, Etc. also boasts a strongly stated business philosophy of commitment to quality merchandise and low prices to ensure customer satisfaction and repeat business. However, the company realizes that each franchisee has individual goals and strengths, and should be allowed the freedom to reach full potential.

It is estimated that Americans spend $6 billion a year on plants. Even if only a small fraction of these purchases fall victim to "brown thumbs," there is still an enormous market for providing greenery that doesn't need constant maintenance. Before long, flora from Silk Plants, Etc. may be "sprouting" on windowsills nationwide.

SOUPER MARKET NICHE
Soup Exchange

The traditional soup kitchen never had it this good: six soup varieties, a 60-item salad bar, fresh fruit, and fresh-baked bread. Soup Exchange restaurants offer this variety every day of the year, catering to the health-conscious, dieters, or anyone who wants a "light" meal. The "light" concept extends to the decor as well, which is airy and spacious, and to the check, averaging $6 for a satisfying meal.

Soup Exchange restaurants grew out of Southern California, where eating light has long been a trend. Scott King and John Turnbull, both food-service veterans, wanted an establishment that combined the speed of a fast-food outlet with the relaxed atmosphere of a traditional restaurant. In 1976, the first Soup Exchange restaurant was set up buffet-style where customers could have as much of any item as they chose. The restaurant was designed with an emphasis on decor, using an abundance of plants and quality furniture and fittings to create a comfortable ambiance, belying its low-priced appeal. The buffet-style serving arrangement offered substantial savings on labor, which constitutes a large expense for table-service restaurants. This concept proved to be a success and was spread to four more company-owned Soup Exchange restaurants within the next nine years.

In 1985, Soup & Salad Systems Incorporated (SASS) was organized as a publicly-held concern to operate several company-owned Soup Exchange restaurants, and to sell franchises for future outlets. SASS based their franchise plans on the belief that since each restaurant required a fairly high investment, franchisees with the resources to open multiple units would be a better risk and could manage each unit more efficiently than a single-store franchisee. The only question was how readily they could locate such multiple-unit operators, but any doubts they may have had were quickly assuaged. By early 1987, 13 Southern California territories had been sold to franchisees who promised to build a total of 48 units. In fact, so popular had the franchise proved, SASS bought back the first two territories they had sold and resold them to other buyers at higher prices! The SASS growth plan calls for eight franchised and five company-owned units by early 1988, with 150 total units (120 of them franchised) by 1991.

Competition within the restaurant business is intense. Any new restaurant finds local competition in all price ranges and in a wide variety of ethnic and regional varieties. Soup Exchange restaurants have been able to succeed by emphasizing a health-conscious image and a moderate price, a combination that few others are able to match.

Studies by restaurant trade publications have shown that the fastest-growing age group in the U.S., 35 to 44, is increasingly health-conscious and is eating lighter, including higher consumption of soup and salads. The same age group is also rapidly becoming more affluent, with more disposable income to spend in restaurants. Soup Exchange restaurants are well-positioned to capitalize on the combination of these two trends and to continue growth nationwide.

Franchising and the Law

When he was a young college-campus pizzeria owner and manager, Tom Monaghan's biggest concern was getting pizza deliveries out before the dorms closed—not the legalities of his restaurant's name, nor the possibility of debts and bankruptcy, nor whether he could require all of his handful of restaurants to purchase the same supplies. But each of those legal problems surfaced as his Domino's Pizza chain grew, and each one threatened to ruin both the chain and its founder. Monaghan now admits that he knew very little about business when his company began, but he eventually learned to keep a close watch on "the whole operation." The moral is clear—in the scheme of the whole operation, regulations and laws are critically important.

If you are seriously considering franchising as a means of expanding your business, you should be aware that as a franchisor your activities are likely to be regulated far more than they have ever been before. Moreover, the laws that will affect you are *in addition to* those that govern companies not involved in the sale of a franchise or business opportunity. It will be extremely useful, then, for you to learn something about how the franchise laws came about and how they will affect you and your business.

Flagrant early abuses

Although franchising has become generally accepted by businesspeople and the public alike, for a small segment of the population it retains a somewhat unfavorable image, incurred, in part, during the 1960s and early 1970s when a number of dubious sellers of franchises cheated investors and consumers. A few of these franchising swindles or mismanagements became front-page news, with stories of people being bilked of their life savings and tarnishing the names of often unsuspecting backers, notably entertainment figures such as Minnie Pearl and Jerry Lewis. Minnie Pearl franchises were essentially fast-food chicken restaurants. Pearl, a popular country-music personality, lent her name to the enterprise, but was not substantially involved in the business. The restaurants failed because the backers hoped to open a large number of restaurants in a short time, but did not establish a strong, standardized operations format for the restaurants once they opened. Jerry Lewis movie theaters were another example of a celebrity endorsement—again, virtually in name only—of a franchise without a comprehensive business plan. Opened at a time when movie theaters were suffering from the competition of television, the franchise quickly folded.

One franchise failure that received a fairly large amount of media coverage—including an investigative report by the television show, "60 Minutes"—was that of Wild Bill's, a hamburger franchise that swindled many hopeful franchisees. The promoters opened one restaurant, then sold franchises for many others, which were never opened because there was no real support forthcoming from the franchisor. These promoters were excellent salesmen, as Mike Wallace of "60 Minutes" learned when he interviewed one of the people who lost their savings investing in a non-existent Wild Bill's franchise. The interviewee, a professional with an understanding of business, when asked by Wallace how he could have been fooled, replied, "If you had been there, you would have bought it too."

In addition to these widely publicized abuses of franchising, the formative years of franchising often saw an emphasis by some franchisors on selling the franchise, and not on the product or service to be franchised. Innocently or by design, many franchisors and franchisees encountered a number of problems with misunderstandings, miscalculations, misrepresentations, and even out-and-out fraud.

State laws

In 1971, in response to a growing number of legal irregularities in franchising, California enacted the first state law pertaining specifically to franchise registration. Throughout the 1970s and early 1980s, other states followed suit, and at this writing, the 14 states listed below (and one Canadian province, Alberta) have adopted rules and regulations requiring that franchisors submit extensive information about the nature of the franchise offering and the history of the people who are making the offer, prior to offering and selling their franchise. This process is commonly called "registration" and the 14 states that require registration are known in the industry as "registration states." In any of these states, you will be required to register (with some exceptions) if one or more of the following conditions occur:

1. The offer is made from the state;
2. The offer is received from the state;
3. The offer is accepted in the state;
4. The franchisee is domiciled in the state;
5. The franchisee resides in the state;
6. The franchisee's business will be located in the state.

Conceivably, if you represent an Illinois-based company and you meet at an airport in New York someone who is a resident of Maryland and who wants to discuss buying a franchise that will be located in California, then you may have to be registered in all four states.

Registration States

California	New York
Hawaii	North Dakota
Illinois	Rhode Island
Indiana	South Dakota
Maryland	Virginia
Michigan	Washington
Minnesota	Wisconsin

Registration states treat the sale of franchises much as they would the sale of securities, which means, among other things, that the franchisor must submit the information to be disclosed in a format approved by the states. This document is generally referred to as the "disclosure statement," or more formally as the "offering circular." Often, the offering circular and the franchise agreement will be cross-checked at the state level to see that they are consistent with one another and that they are both in compliance with the laws of their states. A few states that do not have franchise laws do have business opportunity laws. Some franchise offerings will trigger these laws, but compliance with them will generally be less complicated than in registration states. The laws of the following states are most likely to trigger compliance by franchisors:

Connecticut	North Carolina
Florida	South Carolina
Georgia	Texas
Maine	

In remaining states, where neither franchise nor business opportunity laws apply, franchise documents need not be filed with state agencies. Nevertheless in all states before selling a franchise, the franchisor must provide prospective franchisees with an offering circular prepared in accordance with Federal Trade Commission or Uniform Franchise Offering Circular (see below) guidelines, with all relevant agreements and financial statements attached, and according to a prescribed timetable. In addition, of course, the franchisor must meet any other specific requirements imposed by these states.

The UFOC and the FTC rule

The Uniform Franchise Offering Circular (UFOC) was created and adopted in the mid-1970s to meet the needs of the states that required disclosure on the part of franchisors. Essentially, its rules require that franchisors furnish prospective franchisees with very specific information about the franchisor, the business, and the terms of the franchise relationship.

The FTC guidelines came about as a result of years of investigation and work by various Senate committees and by the Federal Trade Commission on a number of franchising bills. Formally titled "Disclosure Requirements and Prohibitions Concerning Franchising and Business Opportunity Ventures," the FTC Rule was finally approved in December, 1978, and became effective in October, 1979. For the first time, disclosure by franchisors became mandatory in all states, not simply in the registration states and states with business opportunity laws. In addition to providing a format for disclosure (although not one as comprehensive as the UFOC), the FTC Rule defines the type of business relationship that is considered a franchise and exempts, among others, such relationships as single-trademark licenses and membership in retailer-owned cooperatives.

The federal government's attempt, with the FTC Rule, to regulate franchising activity did not diminish the states' authority to do so, and was, in fact, stated to be a minimum standard upon which states could add additional protection as they saw fit. The Rule allows franchisors to comply with the Uniform Franchise Offering Circular in lieu of the FTC format document, provided that either the FTC document or the UFOC is followed in its entirety.

The penalties for failing to comply with the FTC Rule are severe, with up to $10,000 per violation. In one case, a heating and air conditioning franchisor and one of its officers settled an FTC allegation of franchise disclosure rule violations and misrepresentations by agreeing to pay $3 million in consumer redress and over $1 million in civil penalties. In another, the FTC obtained a permanent injunction and a judgement for nearly $1 million against an automobile parts franchisor. The charge: false earnings claims, misrepresentation of available services, and failure to make required disclosures. In addition, states can punish criminal violations, such as fraud, by imprisonment. In 1980, the president of Pie Tree, a Pennsylvania restaurant franchise, was sentenced by an Illinois court to three years in prison for selling a franchise without an offering circular and without registering in the state, as well as for defrauding a franchisee. Most state franchise laws also provide for a private course of action to recover damages.

As stated above, when selling franchises in states that do not require registration, a franchisor need only prepare an offering circular that meets the requirements of the FTC rule or the UFOC. Both documents require extensive disclosure of various facts pertaining to the franchisor's general business history. A franchisor—with the help of an experienced franchise attorney—needs to determine which of these disclosure formats will be less complicated or burdensome, given the nature and history of its business.

Although the UFOC is more comprehensive in its requirements than the FTC, both formats call for disclosure—with differing levels of detail—of a wide range of information. A properly prepared UFOC, in fact, includes data on each of the following topics:

1. The franchisor and any predecessors
2. Identity and business experience of persons affiliated with the franchisor or franchise sales agents
3. Litigation
4. Bankruptcy
5. Franchisee's initial franchise fee or other initial payment

6. Other fees
7. Franchisee's initial investment
8. Obligations of franchisee to purchase or lease from designated sources
9. Obligations of franchisee to purchase or lease in accordance with specifications or from approved suppliers
10. Financing arrangements
11. Obligations of the franchisor; other supervision, assistance, or services
12. Territorial rights
13. Trademarks, service marks, trade names, logotypes, and commercial symbols
14. Patents and copyrights
15. Obligation of the franchisee to participate in the actual operation of the franchise business
16. Restrictions on goods and services offered by franchisee
17. Renewal, termination, repurchase, modification, and assignment of the agreements and related information
18. Arrangements with public figures
19. Actual, average, projected, or forecasted franchisee sales, profits, or earnings
20. Information regarding franchises of the franchisor
21. Financial statements
22. Contracts
23. Receipt of offering circular

It should be noted that under both the Rule and UFOC requirements if you have declared bankruptcy or been a principal officer in a company that has declared bankruptcy, the facts and dates of the circumstances and proceedings must be disclosed if they occurred within a specified period of time. Likewise, a litigation history of listed and "material" actions for the franchisor's principal officers or partners—covering the previous 10 years under the UFOC and seven years under the FTC, plus any pending actions (except in California)—must be included. By omitting or materially altering this information—whether intentionally or accidentally—a franchisor could be severely penalized (as stated above—up to $10,000 *per violation*).

While the laws governing franchise offerings were enacted to regulate and protect the entire industry, it is clear that the disclosure laws are in place mainly to inform and benefit potential franchisees. However, *complying*—correctly and thoroughly—with these laws is to the benefit of franchisors. Proper compliance will not only help avoid illegalities and penalties, but can also be the important first step in educating the franchisee in the background, rules, and regulations of your franchise system.

The standardization and acceptance of these rules—coupled with the pioneering and ongoing efforts of the state laws—has diminished the occurrence of fraudulent franchise offerings. Today, both franchisors and potential franchisees are better informed about the industry's legal requirements, and, consequently, the tarnished image of the 1960s has been replaced by well-regulated professionalism.

The franchise agreement

Federal laws and the laws of many states require that every franchise company submit to its prospective franchisees a document that specifies in detail the terms under which franchisor and franchisee will do business together. Perhaps no one part of the franchise development process is as important to the ultimate success of the franchise as the drafting of this document, commonly known as the franchise agreement. This agreement must describe explicitly the entire extent of your relationship with franchisees, outlining the terms and considerations by which you will agree to allow them to operate your franchise, use your trademark, and sell your products or services. By establishing standards of operation, the agreement helps to ensure uniformity throughout the franchise system. It also provides clearly defined guidelines by which a franchise can be terminated.

It is essential that an attorney who understands franchising and is familiar with your business prepare this agreement, and it's equally important for you to participate in the development of the agreement because it is you who are most knowledgeable about the circumstances and requirements of your business. This is not the time to save money by copying a "standard" franchise agreement or for "boilerplate" legal work. Each franchise agreement should be as unique as the business it represents. It is the cornerstone of your franchise relationship, and it must be thorough enough to provide both parties with a clear understanding of that relationship. By all means, you want to avoid the unfortunate situation that many franchisors encounter when a problem arises with their franchisees. They rush to look at their agreements to see if the situation is covered, only to find that it isn't and there is no easy legal remedy. The franchise agreement should also be fair to the franchisee. A well-drafted document will protect the franchisee and will meet with minimal objections from his or her attorney.

Over the years, franchise attorneys in our firm in conjunction with attorneys of our clients have drafted hundreds of franchise agreements and have analyzed hundreds more. The following outline touches briefly on the most important points a well-written franchise agreement should address:

1. Appointment and franchise fee
2. Location
   A. Right to approve sites
   B. Right to prime lease
   C. Tie lease to franchise agreement
   D. Plans and specifications
   E. Equipment must conform to specifications
3. Proprietary marks
   A. Use of name
   B. Contest of name
   C. Notification to franchisor of other's use of name
   D. Conformance to operation manual
   E. Use products, systems, and supplies as specified
   F. Signage requirements

4. Training and assistance
   A. Must complete training
   B. Start-up assistance
5. Franchisor's ongoing operations assistance
   A. Continuing advisory service
   B. Promotional materials and bulletins, marketing developments, products, and techniques
6. Advertising
   A. Approval of all advertising copy, material, packaging, and promotional materials
   B. Establishment of national advertising fund
   C. Local advertising
   D. Co-op advertising
   E. Grand opening advertising requirements
7. Operating manual
   A. Must adhere
   B. Confidential
   C. Property of franchisor
8. Confidential information
   A. Know-how, techniques, and product formulas are trade secrets
   B. Protection necessary
9. Maintenance and repairs
   A. Maintain interior and exterior
   B. Create fund for refurbishing
10. Accounting and records
    A. Must keep complete records as prescribed
    B. Provide for reports
    C. Allow for inspection of records
    D. Provide for audited statements
    E. Weekly reports and payments of royalty
11. Standards of quality and performance
    A. Establish need for uniformity
    B. Provide for purchases which conform to specifications
    C. Dictate type, quality, and quantity of purchases

12. Modification of system
    A. Establish right of franchisor to modify
    B. Prohibit franchisees from unauthorized modification
13. Continuing services and royalty fee
    A. Establish royalty
        i. Determine program necessary to provide ongoing support and consulting service
        ii. Project total direct and indirect costs of providing continuing services
        iii. Establish percentage of royalty and continuing service fee to provide for costs and reasonable return for use of franchisor's name, concept, and system
        iv. Ensure payment of royalties
14. Insurance
    A. Protection for franchisee and franchisor
    B. Establish amounts of protection necessary
        i. Workman's compensation
        ii. General liability—products and bodily injury
        iii. Property damage
15. Term
    A. Determine term
        i. Renewal and termination provisions must comply with laws
        ii. Renewal conditioned on updating image of facility
        iii. Coordinate with lease
        iv. Long term
            a. Insures royalty longer to franchisor
            b. More security for franchisee
        v. Short term
            a. Adjust royalty upward if desired
            b. Eliminate undesirable franchisees
            c. Allows for earlier execution of new terms and conditions

16. Covenants
    A. Establish restrictions of franchisee's ability to compete, divert business, hire away employees, and divulge secrets—subject to state and antitrust laws
    B. Franchisor's remedies
17. Termination and defaults
    A. Bankruptcy
    B. Notice to cure—varies from state to state
    C. Failure to pay royalties of fees
    D. Failure to submit reports or financial data
    E. Vacation or abandonment of premises
    F. Failure to comply with franchise agreement
    G. Injury to system and marks
    H. Loss of license
18. Rights and duties of parties upon expiration or termination
    A. Franchisee must pay all sums owing
    B. Franchisee must cease using name
    C. Franchisor's right to purchase physical assets
    D. Franchisor's right to signage and items identified by marks
19. Commencement and hours of operation
    A. Specify when agreement commences
    B. Determine hours and days of operation short of agency relationship
20. Transferability of interest
    A. Provide conditions under which franchisee can sell
        i. Transfer fee
        ii. Right of approval
        iii. Payment of fees and sums
        iv. Not unreasonably withheld
        v. Require training of new franchisee
21. Death of franchisee
    A. Survivors can apply to continue
    B. Survivors can sell
    C. Franchisor can buy assets and real estate

D. Provide formula for buy-out

22. Right of first refusal
    A. Franchisee must notify franchisor of bona fide offer
    B. Franchisor can buy at same price as buyer

23. Operation in event of disability or death
    A. Franchisor's right to operate
    B. Save harmless

24. Taxes and permits
    A. Require payment of taxes, assessment, liens, equipment, and previous accounts
    B. Require compliance with all federal, state, and local laws
    C. Require obtaining of all permits, certificates, and licenses necessary

25. Independent contractor
    A. Not agent, partner, or employee of franchisor
    B. Can't incur liability to franchisor
    C. Franchisee bears cost of defense of claims

26. Non-waiver
    A. Non-enforcement by franchisor is not a waiver
    B. Receipt of payments not waiver

27. Notice
    A. Manner of notice
    B. Date of notice

28. Liability for breach enforcement
    A. Payment of costs, attorneys' fee by party in default

29. Entire agreement
    A. Overrides any previous agreements
    B. Provides for amendments, changes, or variance only if in writing.

30. Severability
    A. Each section of agreement is severable
    B. Franchisor can terminate agreement if parts found illegal affect basic consideration of agreement

31. Applicable law
    A. Specifies which states' laws apply
32. Arbitration (where and when applicable)
    A. Provides for selection of arbiters
    B. Binding arbitration
33. Franchisee acknowledges receipt of FTC or UFOC documents
34. Franchisee
    A. Define term "franchisee" to include successors and all parties of interest
35. Caveat
    A. Disclaimers as to claims made
    B. Franchisee assumes risks
    C. Success of business cannot be guaranteed
    D. Success of business also depends on franchisee's ability
    E. Disclaimer about FTC rule and disclosure

All of the subjects mentioned above are important, but some are less obviously important than others:

Maintenance and repair. Franchise agreements we have seen frequently omit a clause that requires the franchisee to maintain his unit to a certain minimum standard, as specified in the operations manual. The clause may allow the franchisor to make necessary repairs, if the franchisee does not do so, at the franchisee's expense. It may also incorporate a fund, made up of periodic contributions by the franchisee, for refurbishing the franchisee's unit.

Insurance. Many agreements address insurance provisions minimally or not at all. The franchise agreement should require the franchisee, at the very least, to have liability, workman's compensation, and property insurance and specify minimum coverages, with the franchisor as co-insured receiving a copy of the policy and any notice of cancellation. The franchisor may wish to recommend an insurance company (frequently the franchisor can negotiate lower rates based on volume), although the franchisee has the right to select his own carrier so long as the policy meets the coverage requirements of the franchisor. Moreover, you may want to provide that if the franchisee does not obtain proper coverage, the franchisor may do so and be immediately reimbursed by the franchisee.

Training. The franchisor's training program is the last stage of the process of qualifying a franchisee. It is important that the agreement state that the franchisee must successfully complete that program, and that if he does not do so the franchisor may terminate the franchise agreement and retain a specified percentage of the franchise fee.

Advertising. The franchise agreement should require the franchisee to use only advertising materials developed or approved by the franchisor, and state clearly how the materials are to be submitted for approval and to whom. Many franchisors require that franchisees contribute to an advertising fund of joint benefit to all franchisees that is administered by the franchisor, and the agreement should specify to whom the money should be paid (perhaps the franchisor's in-house advertising agency) and how often.

Transferability of interest. In the event that the franchisee wishes to sell his franchise, a clause in the agreement should stipulate provisions under which that can be done, including: 1. Approval of the new buyer by the franchisor; 2. Successful completion of training by the new buyer; 3. Payment of a transfer and training fee to the franchisor; and 4. Payment in advance of all fees to the franchisor by the franchisee. The agreement should indicate that the franchisor will not unreasonably withhold approval of the buyer, and it may give the franchisor right of first refusal to buy the franchise at whatever price has been offered. Lastly, the agreement should specify on what terms, if the franchisee dies, the survivors can operate the business or sell it, and on what terms the franchisor can acquire it.

Acknowledgement of receipt of documents. The federal rule states that the prospective franchisee must be presented with an offering circular 10 business days before the execution of a franchise agreement or payment of any money and a completed franchise agreement five business days before fees can be taken from an applicant. The salesman should obtain a receipt for these documents, but receipts are known to have been lost. If the agreement itself states that the franchisee acknowledges receiving the documents the required number of days in advance, a franchisee who subsequently fails in his business will have extreme difficulty prevailing in a lawsuit against a franchisor on the spurious grounds that the franchisor accepted his money without the proper waiting period or disclosure of required information.

These and other "small" details of a well-prepared franchise agreement could conceivably save the franchisor embarassment, expense, and even a catastrophic lawsuit.

All of the issues mentioned in the above outline should be discussed with your attorney. But even should you be fortunate to find an attorney experienced in representing franchisors (most of the few attorneys with franchise law experience have been involved exclusively with franchisees), you should not expect your attorney alone to make your business decisions for you. Do you want to go on the prime lease? This decision, like so many others, will be based upon your financial abilities, the importance of location to your concept, the degree of control you wish to exercise over franchisees, and other non-legal considerations.

In closing, we suggest that franchisors begin preparing for a lawsuit the day they sign the franchise agreement. It sounds cynical, but in today's business climate, with its increasing reliance on litigation, the warning is valid. Franchisors should carefully document everything they do for their franchisees, keeping comprehensive files and records that indicate every phone call, every dispute that's resolved, every visit to the franchise (even casual ones), and every instance in which the franchisee is not in compliance. Of course, if the franchisee is not in compliance, you should notify him or her immediately or you may not be able to enforce compliance later.

Frequently asked questions

Even after studying the FTC rule, the UFOC, and assorted state laws, many franchisors have specific questions about real-world interpretations and day-to-day implications of these myriad laws. In our experience, the following are among the most commonly asked legal questions about franchising:

1. Can I require a franchisee to purchase products from me?

Usually not, but there are exceptions. One key is whether the franchisor's trademark is so closely associated with the product in question that it would be a misrepresentation to offer anything else. Baskin-Robbins is well within its rights to require that Baskin-Robbins franchisees buy Baskin-Robbins ice cream. Customers, after all, expect it. A less obvious case in point is the requirement by a California franchisor, Soup Exchange, that franchisees buy the franchisor's salad and spice mix. The franchisor believes that its special recipe is a proprietary formula and trade secret and contributes significantly to the success of its program. On the other hand, a franchisor can require a franchisee to buy products of certain quality without actually selling those products to the franchisee. Kentucky Fried Chicken, for example, requires that franchisees buy the "secret blend of herbs and spices" for the coating mix from designated distributors.

Cases in which franchisees have accused franchisors of using their power to force franchisees to buy products from them are known as "tying" cases. The courts have ruled that some tying requirements in franchisor/franchisee relationships violate antitrust laws. However, the courts *have* recognized that the very nature of franchising may lend itself to certain instances where required purchases of products and services will not be an illegal tie. An *illegal* tie occurs when a franchisor requires that franchisees buy a secondary product in order to be allowed to purchase the primary product of the franchisor. For example, many oil companies once would provide gasoline only to service stations that purchased tires, batteries, and other accessories. After a rash of these "TBA" cases (for "tires, batteries, and accessories") in the 1950s and 1960s, this practice was found to be illegal under the Sherman Anti-Trust Act. Chicken Delight franchisees argued against having to buy napkins, wrapping papers, and boxes bearing the Chicken Delight trademark from the franchisor—at higher prices than they could have paid for the same items elsewhere—and the court also upheld their claims by finding this to be an illegal tie.

2. How do I answer the prospective franchisee who asks, "How much money can I make from your franchise?"

Stories abound about the franchisor who reportedly wrote a dollar amount on a cocktail napkin and showed it to a prospective franchisee in answer to the question, then pocketed the napkin, which was never seen again. However, a few of those napkin-type notes have turned up in court, and as we have stated, the penalties for misrepresentation can be severe. Another misleading practice involved showing a prospective franchisee a sheet of paper that had on it a graph showing that at sales of $300,000, the franchisee would earn $50,000; at sales of $500,000, the earnings would be $100,000 a year; and with $700,000 in sales, the franchisee could expect earnings of $150,000, when in fact there were no units in operation, or there were a few but none with sales even approaching $200,000. The response by legislatures has been to establish specific guidelines for earnings claims based upon solid financial criteria.

In 1987, the willingness of the FTC to back up its ruling regarding earnings claims was made abundantly clear to the franchise community. Responding to an FTC complaint that they had misrepresented earnings and profits of its franchisees, Comprehensive Accounting Corp., a franchisor with more than 350 units, signed a consent decree and, without admitting it broke the law, agreed to pay back franchisees up to $3.5 million in fees. The company had been charged with:

- Failing to indicate whether the contracts of franchises being cited for earnings had similar terms to those being offered.

- Using improper accounting methods in determining average earnings and profits.

- Failing to disclose that the sample group used in computing average earnings and profits excluded franchisees who had dropped out of the program.

Both the UFOC and the FTC guidelines contain provisions that describe how claims of actual, projected, or forecasted franchisee sales, profits, or earnings can be presented, if the franchisor so desires. It's a difficult decision to make for the franchisor. On the one hand, being able to tell a prospective franchise buyer what his or her earnings might total can be an effective sales tool. However, franchisors are sometimes reluctant to make claims that imply a promise to the franchisee that he or she should do as well as the projected earnings. The result can be dissatisfaction and unhappiness (even litigation) if the franchisee's earnings ultimately do not meet what was "promised."

3. Can I prevent my franchisees from doing business outside of their territories?

That depends upon the type of franchise you are offering. If your franchisee operates from a fixed location, as is the case with most retail businesses, you as franchisor cannot legally prevent your franchisee from promoting and selling his goods and services to anyone who seeks to buy them. However, if a portion or all of your franchisee's business is not location based—if, for example, the franchisee operates a sales force in a previously assigned and protected territory—then you may greatly limit that franchisee's ability to promote or sell outside the territory. Or, at the very least, you may provide that franchise owners of adjacent territories be compensated for sales made by other franchisees within their territories according to a predetermined formula.

The best way to keep a franchisee within his or her assigned territory is to establish and enforce specific guidelines for development of that territory, specifying, for example, the number of sales calls the franchisee must make per day and the number of promotional brochures he must send to all prospective customers in the territory per month or per year. Under the concept of "area of primary responsibility," the courts have held that activities such as those mentioned above can be enforced.

4. Can I set the prices that my franchisees will charge their customers?

No. The courts have found such price-fixing to be anti-competitive. The most you can do is suggest guidelines for the prices your franchisees ask for the goods or services they sell. (However, franchisors may obtain the agreement of franchisees to participate in special regional or nationwide promotions, offering products or services at special, standardized prices.)

5. Can I sell goods and services for different prices to different franchisees?

No, unless factors such as delivery costs or quantity purchases are involved, but these must be applied equally to all franchisees.

6. Can I compete with my franchisees in the same territory?

Only if your franchisee has not already been granted an exclusive territory in the franchise agreement, and if your competition does not cause him economic injury. Under exclusive territorial arrangements, a franchisee has the sole right to open franchises in a particular area—a state, county, city, or whatever region the contract specifies. Most territorial arrangements now cover no more than a radius of a few miles—or, in a big city, a few blocks. Since 1969, McDonald's has limited most of its territorial arrangements to the street address of the franchise.

7. Can I terminate a franchisee for not following my prescribed businesss format?

Yes, within reason. You must show good cause for such an action, and to reduce the threat of litigation, those causes should be spelled out in your franchise agreement and in your operations manuals. Your franchisees can't follow your system if they don't know exactly what it is. McDonald's successfully terminated a franchisee in Paris in 1982 after repeatedly notifying him that the restaurant did not meet McDonald's standards for cleanliness. Ample time was given to correct the violations, and when he did not comply, the franchise was terminated. This termination was upheld by a court decision strongly in McDonald's favor. More difficult issues arise when franchisees assert that their changes reflect their own expertise in responding to a local market. Such cases may involve slight changes in operating hours to fit a particular area or neighborhood or regional changes in a restaurant's menu. (Such a change could include replacing pork or beef dishes on a menu out of deference to the religious and/or dietary customs of large portions of a restaurant's clientele.) Here, too, the courts—if it comes to that—will look for the degree to which the franchisor's demands are reasonable.

8. Can I prevent my franchisee from taking down his sign after a few years (to avoid paying royalties) and operating the business with my system without paying me?

It depends on the state the franchisee is located in and the kind of franchise program in place. For business-format franchises, if the legal documents are properly drafted, there will be "in term" and "post term" restricted covenants that will prevent franchisees from operating a similar business for a certain period of time within a defined geographic area. The enforceability of such clauses changes from state to state. For example, some states say a reasonable restraint is to prevent the franchisee from being in the business for two years within 25 miles. Other states require less restraint in order for the covenant to be enforceable. (Conversion franchises are a different—and trickier—matter. These franchisees have generally already been established in the particular business before becoming franchisees, and they usually face less restriction—again, these vary from state to state.)

9. When can I legally offer my franchises for sale?

To offer a franchise for sale, you must first have a properly prepared franchise agreement and offering circular as described above. Depending on the domicile of your company and your buyer, where the unit will be located, and where the sale will take place, you may also have to register the franchise in appropriate states.

You must provide every buyer or every prospect with a copy of the offering circular at the first face-to-face meeting at which there is a serious discussion of the sale of this business opportunity or franchise. Even then, you must wait a minimum of 10 business days before you accept any money and before the franchise or related agreements are executed. The agreement must be completed five business days before the franchise accepts it.

10. Are there conditions under which I can sell a franchise for different fees to different people?

Yes, a few. You can charge a lower franchise fee to someone who knows your business, as opposed to a complete neophyte who requires extensive training. When setting up your franchise program, you may also state your intention to sell a specified number of franchises at an "introductory" price, noting that you intend to increase the price at a specified date or after a certain number of franchises have been sold. There are also instances in which you might sell a multi-unit or subfranchisor program (which we'll discuss in more detail later), offering a discount, in effect, for buying more than one unit or a larger territory. However, the key is that all potential buyers must be offered the same opportunity to buy a franchise at that price under those same conditions.

These are some of the most significant legal issues that confront any new franchisor. They illustrate, for one thing, how vital is the need for well-crafted documents by specialists in franchise law. On the other hand, legal issues should not dominate your decision-making process. You need not be concerned about disclosure so long as you answer all questions honestly. Above all, do not permit legal issues to drive your decision whether or not to franchise; that is a business decision and must be based upon the various criteria we discussed in earlier chapters. Finally, the cost of complying with the franchise laws may not be as high as you suppose. We will discuss these and other costs of franchising later in the book.

The fact is that most franchise laws have been a boon to franchising. They have made franchising a dangerous game for the few people whose principal interest is in making a fast buck and moving on. In our opinion, the cost of complying with these laws is well worth the improved reputation of franchising and increased security for franchisees they have brought about.

Putting It All Together

Now that you understand the advantages of franchising and perceive how those advantages relate to your business, you may have decided that your business is franchisable. You may also be persuaded, as we are, that franchising offers greater potential for growth than other expansion systems. But it is one thing to arrive at these conclusions and quite another to take the irrevocable steps that lead to becoming a franchisor.

Before you do that, you need to have a clear understanding of the commitment you must make in time, effort, and money. In particular, you need to fully appreciate how important planning, administration, and franchise experience will be to a successful franchise program, and how becoming a franchisor differs from the free-wheeling entrepreneurship that some business owners— and especially founders—may have been accustomed to.

Even if you have proved yourself as a corporate CEO, you ought to be aware of the multi-faceted aspects of franchise development before you make a final decision.

Franchise development, then, is the subject of this chapter. What decisions must you make, what documents and materials will you need, what help will you require, and what will it cost to put together a well-rounded franchise program?

We will address these questions in two parts: strategic planning and documentation.

Strategic planning

Review and Research

Strategic planning really consists of decision-making. But before intelligent decisions can be made concerning the form of your franchise program, it will be useful to examine the structure of other franchise programs—especially those of your competitors, if any. In particular, you will want to know: 1. What investment is being required of the franchisees; 2. What services are being provided; 3. What franchise fees, royalties, and advertising fees are being assessed; and 4. How the territory is defined. It may also be helpful to know the duration of the contracts signed between your competitors and their franchisees, or, in other words, the terms of their franchise agreements. The U.S. Department of Commerce's *Franchise Opportunities Handbook* will list most—though perhaps not all—of your competitors and will give some of this information. But for a detailed review you should obtain the offering circulars of these companies. The easiest way to get an offering circular for any franchisor is to write to the appropriate agency of any state where the franchisor is registered to sell franchises. These documents are, by law, available to the public.

Franchise categories

By the time you are ready to franchise, you will undoubtedly know the category of franchising best suited to your company. These categories are, as you will remember from Chapter 1:

1. Business-format
2. Product distributorship
3. Conversion

But the fact that one of these categories is better suited to your business than the other two may not necessarily exclude the others. In particular, some franchisors combine the business-format and conversion categories. In addition to functioning as traditional business-format franchisors—enlisting as franchisees people who are new to their business—they also accept as franchisees owners of existing similar businesses who are willing to change their business' name to that of the franchisor. But while traditional conversion franchises, such as real estate brokerages, require only that the franchisee adopt the franchisor's name and join in marketing efforts, these companies are requiring that the conversion franchisee also adopt their business system. This tactic has the obvious advantage of eliminating a great deal of the time and trouble involved in recruiting and training start-up franchisees, but it usually means that a lower franchise fee must be charged as well.

There are other disadvantages to recruiting—or trying to recruit—franchisees from among established businesses. History has shown that franchisees who know nothing whatever about a franchisor's specific business but are ready and willing to be taught often are more successful than franchisees who must be convinced that their previous methods were inadequate. The typical response of many a business owner (and competitor) is, "Who are you to tell me how to run my business?" Even the most talented salesman will have difficulty overcoming that kind of resistance. Such offerings usually do best when the advantages of affiliation with a larger entity—advertising, purchasing discounts, etc.—can be clearly demonstrated.

Franchise Type

Once your franchising category has been determined, the next step is to decide on the type of franchise or franchises to be sold.

Again, there are three to be considered:

1. Individual franchise. A franchise awarded to an individual, group of individuals, or a company for one business unit to be operated at one location or one geographically-defined area.

2. Multi-unit or area development franchise. A franchise awarded to an individual, group, or company for a territory in which more than one unit will be established *and* operated by the franchisee.

3. Subfranchise. A franchise awarded to an individual, group, or company for a territory in which several individual franchises will be sold, usually by the subfranchisor, and usually operated under the subfranchisor's administration and supervision.

The question every new franchisor must ask himself or herself is: Do I want to offer one, two, or three of these options to prospective franchisees? The answer to that question will depend upon both the business characteristics of the franchisor and the franchisor's goals.

Generally speaking (although by no means absolutely), the smaller and more expensive the individual unit, the more difficult multi-unit or subfranchising will be. However, even when low-priced, easy-to-establish, highly clusterable franchises are being offered, we usually recommend that the new franchisor limit sales to individual units in the early stages of the franchise program. For one thing, the buyer of the individual unit is likely to be easier to find and, once found, easier to deal with than the more sophisticated multi-unit buyer. Then, too, the franchisor must also undergo a "training" period as he or she learns first-hand about the realities of franchise relationships—and it is generally better to keep things as simple as possible until that learning period is over.

Of course, as always, the resources and sophistication of the franchisor may dictate a different approach. Merle Harmon's Fan Fair, a company that started with just four units, all located in regional malls, chose to grow with multi-unit sales and succeeded—although not without a period of retrenchment and consolidation after the first franchise territories were sold. And in cases where rapid market penetration and/or saturation is dictated by competitive conditions, multi-unit or subfranchising from the outset may be essential.

Multi-unit territories

Unquestionably, the sale of multiple units to a franchisee *who is ready to open them immediately* is the most rapid means of franchise expansion. But for a company new to franchising that has only a few units (or perhaps only one or two) it may not be easy to attract affluent buyers capable of large cash outlays.

Moreover, multi-unit development can actually be slower than growth by individual units if the units in the multi-unit territories are not developed simultaneously. And the fact is that many multiple-unit buyers either are not capable of opening all of their units at once or do not choose to do so, preferring instead to test the waters with one, then gradually add the additional units.

We strongly recommend that any franchisor require his multi-unit buyer to abide by a performance schedule establishing, say, one unit in his 5-unit territory every year. But even under such an agreement, it will be five years before the territory is fully developed. Meanwhile, your competition may have moved in and your window of opportunity may be lost. In contrast, you might well find that by establishing an individual franchisee in the territory, you can more quickly attract buyers for the other four units in the area.

McDonald's once made the mistake of selling to one person the rights to a territory that included all of Canada. Although the franchisee began to build units, he lacked the resources to develop a territory that large. The competition quickly moved in, bought what would have been prime locations for McDonald's units, and began opening stores. Within a few years, McDonald's recognized its error and bought the rights to the territory back—at 10 times the original price.

As we have noted, the ideal area-development candidate would have the funds to open multiple units on an accelerated schedule, without relying upon the first unit to generate enough cashflow to fund the second, the second to fund the third, etc. This franchisee also should possess a high level of operational expertise, perhaps in a related business. He may operate multiple units of that business, and also have the central payroll, the personnel, and the capital to make this transition. For example, a good prospect for a multi-unit transmission-repair franchise might be someone who already owns five muffler shops or several car washes. Such prospects, unlike many owner/operator prospects, do not buy on an emotional level. They bring in accountants and attorneys and ask questions such as, "How much equity capital do I need to open each unit and what is the internal rate of return on equity over a 5- to 10-year period?"

Subfranchises

Many large franchisors—among them Convenient Food Mart, Budget Rent A Car, and Century 21—have used subfranchising to successfully accelerate growth, especially during highly competitive periods when becoming established in new markets as quickly as possible was of critical importance. Some franchisors use subfranchising to grow, then later buy back territories for the purpose of increasing the number of units in those territories.

The subfranchisor normally does not operate units, other than a single showcase unit with headquarters and training facilities. Instead, he takes a large burden from the franchisor's shoulders by selling individual and multi-unit franchises within his territory, and is generally responsible for training the franchisees and making periodic supervisory visits. In return, he customarily shares in both the franchise fee and royalty paid by the franchisee, usually taking a larger portion than the franchisor.

But subfranchising is not to be undertaken lightly. Franchisors who are quality-control sensitive may not want to abrogate critical responsibilities to a third party. Precision Tune, Inc., an automotive franchise providing quick tune-ups, avoided quality-control problems by limiting its subfranchisors' territories, and requiring that they provide a great deal of specific assistance to their franchisees, especially in site-selection, construction, training, and advertising. Other companies have recruited subfranchisors from among their successful franchisees.

The owner of the Fantastic Sam's haircutting franchise, Sam M. Ross, saw subfranchising as a way to expand rapidly without adding significantly to his staff and overhead costs. In less than five years he increased the number of his units more than sixfold while adding only two people to his payroll. Ross' program generously allows subfranchisors to keep 85 percent of the initial franchise fees and royalties, but even at that greatly reduced percentage, the franchisor's net income has grown steadily. Awarding subfranchisors large shares of the franchise fee and royalties is by no means unusual. Convenient Food Mart allows its subfranchisors to retain 80 percent of the royalties, because subfranchisors provide the bulk of the services and ongoing support.

Incidentally, subfranchisors who sell franchises in their own territories must file registration materials comparable to those required of a franchisor in states that require registration.

Determining income sources

Franchise fees and royalties are the two basic income sources for most franchise programs, but for every franchisor they pose a dilemma. It is of critical importance for the new franchisor to establish fees and royalties low enough so that franchisees with reasonable sale volumes will have little difficulty paying them and making a profit. At the same time, it is imperative that these fees and royalties be high enough to enable the franchisor to provide the services he or she knows franchisees will require. In some cases, of course, other sources of income can have an important bearing on fees and royalties.

Franchise fees

The initial, one-time franchise fee enables the franchisor to recover, in some degree, the costs involved in developing the franchise program, selling the franchise, training the franchisee, and providing support for new franchisees during the start-up period when expenses to the franchisor exceed royalty income. What should your franchisee fee be? Three factors should be considered:

1. The franchisee's return on investment;
2. Your total start-up costs, plus a profit;
3. What competitors in your industry and your investment range charge.

This last factor may be the most important. If the competition in either your industry or your price bracket is heavy, you may find that a relatively low franchise fee is essential to get the running start you need. On the other hand, your business concept may be so attractive and your track record so impressive that you can virtually name your price. One of our clients, Soup Exchange, required an investment in excess of $300,000 per restaurant. We suggested a relatively modest franchisee fee of $22,500, which the client grudgingly accepted. Soup Exchange sold 44 franchises in its first 18 months, then doubled the franchise fee to $45,000. To our surprise—and the client's delight—no perceptible buyer resistance to the new fee was encountered.

Related Costs

The problem of determining franchise fees is directly related to the cost of selling the franchise and providing services that will enable the franchise to get off to a running start and be successful. These services are:

Sales. If you choose the right marketing strategies, select the right media, and following the advice offered in Chapter 9 concerning ad size and placement, you can expect to spend as little as $2,000 for media or related costs for each franchise you sell (except for the first few franchises, which may cost more). In addition, you may have sales commissions to pay—a commission to a staff person might be $2,000-$5,000—plus costs for overhead, employee benefits and support for an in-house sales force. Or, if you decide to use a franchise broker, you may pay as much as 20 to 40 percent of the franchise fee.

Training. You must provide both the personnel to train your franchisees and, perhaps, other people on his staff, as well as a place for the training to take place.

Site selection and lease negotiations. If you agree to assist with these activities, you may be committed to one or more visits to a franchisee's city prior to the opening of a unit. You should not have to assist with the selection of equipment and accessories; they should be listed in your operations manual.

Start-up assistance. Someone from your company needs to be present at the time the franchisee opens for business to help hire and train employees, set up the record-keeping system, and generally get the business on a firm footing. At least a week or two will be required. Thereafter, close monitoring and weekly or semimonthly visits will be required until the franchisee begins building volume and operating at a profit.

Obviously, the specific costs of these services will vary from franchise to franchise. They will also vary depending upon who is chosen to perform the services. The dilemma for every franchisor that accompanies franchise fee decision-making is this: To assure that franchisees are given the best possible training and assistance and thus the optimum opportunity to succeed, the most effective person—and usually the most expensive—must be assigned to those functions. At the same time, royalty revenues from the franchisee in this period will be the lowest they will ever be. Where does money come from to support the high-intensity service upon which the success of the franchise program rests? There are two possible answers: investment capital and franchise fees. The typical franchisor, then, must: 1. Raise the franchise fee and therefore sell fewer units, or 2. Find more investment capital.

Either way, one of the greatest dangers a franchisor faces is to sell too many units too quickly at the start. If you don't provide the proper support and the franchisees fail, your entire program is in jeopardy. Or if, because of inadequate funding, you don't provide proper support and the franchises succeed despite your lack of visibility and meaningful guidance, they will harbor resentment against you for years to come.

Pop-Ins Maid Service is an example of a franchisor that sold too many franchises too fast at franchise fees insufficient to pay the cost of adequate support. In time, lawsuits from franchisees drove the franchisor into bankruptcy, while some franchisees organized and formed a franchise program of their own under a new name.

The entire dilemma of high support costs versus low income is graphically expressed in the chart that follows. The franchisor's expenses per unit will continue to exceed income until they are equaled by franchise fees and royalties and the expense and revenue lines cross. We call this phenomenon the "X-factor."

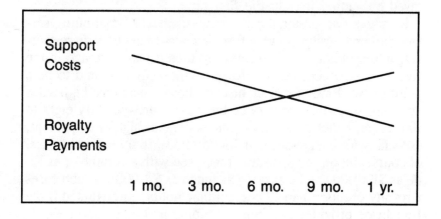

Royalties

As important as setting the right franchise fee is, it is not nearly as critical as establishing the right royalty percentage. The franchise fee will be collected once; royalties come in for as long as the franchise exists. In the early days of franchising, companies such as Red Carpet Realty and Steamatic (an on-location cleaning service franchise) were eager to expand rapidly. At the same time they may have been overly solicitous of franchisee feelings. In any event, they established royalties as low as one or two percent. Before long, the cost of providing services to their franchisees exceeded income flow; but when they sought to raise their royalty rates, the franchisees resisted increases, so services declined. And the decline of services in all such cases impairs the viability of the franchise. On the other hand, ComputerLand, lacking competitors in its early years, established a very high royalty for a franchise that sells low-margin products—eight percent. In time, as competition increased and as margins on computer hardware decreased, franchisees began to grumble. Finally, they organized and forced ComputerLand to lower its royalty to 6.5 percent. A great deal of time, money, and conflict can be saved by getting it right the first time.

Royalties (we prefer the more precise term "continuing service fees and royalties") vary from industry to industry. In restaurants and specialty retail stores, royalties usually average in the five- to six-percent range. However, these figures tend to be a point or two lower for franchisors whose units boast high sales volumes. Royalties for service businesses are typically eight to 10 percent, although we have seen them go as high as 20 percent, especially for businesses with low volumes. In service industries, of course, an owner/operator franchisee with a volume of as little as $100,000 can be earning as much as $70,000; in such cases a royalty of more than 10 percent may not be unwarranted if the franchisor provides continuing training and other services.

The more quality-control sensitive a business is, the more services are required of the franchisor and the higher the royalty income must be for the company to be successful. One way of approaching the royalty question is to look at projected expenses versus projected income. If yours is like many franchises, one field supervisor should be able to service 10 to 25 individual units. (The lower figure is more common in the early stages, when franchisees require the most support.) Assuming a $35,000 salary and an equal amount in back-up expenses for that person, your unit support cost in the field will be $70,000 divided by 10 units, or $7,000. If your average unit has a sales volume of $350,000 and your royalty is six percent, your royalty income per unit, per year will be $21,000, or $210,000 from the ten units.

Of course, these units are likely to open gradually over a period of months and during part of that time royalties will not pay the entire cost of field supervision. But even so, you can see that once an area is fully developed and operating at mature sales volumes, franchising can be a very profitable way to capitalize upon your ingenuity, knowledge, and experience. And you can also see that scattering units all over the country will not produce sufficient royalty income in any market to cover the minimum support costs. For this reason, it is frequently necessary to cluster units.

Royalties are generally paid as a percentage of sales, or sometimes as a minimum fee against a percentage, but in no case should they be a fixed dollar amount. How often should royalties be collected? We recommend weekly, only because it is inconvenient to collect them hourly. We are only half-joking.

Companies that collect these fees monthly are really making their franchisees a loan of the franchisor's money. In the early stages of a franchise program, that kind of beneficence is rarely affordable. But weekly collection is not simply a matter of maintaining cash-flow; it enables the franchisor to monitor franchisees and to respond quickly at the first sign of trouble.

Multi-unit and subfranchise fees and royalties

To encourage multi-unit buyers, you may want to reduce the franchise fee and perhaps the royalty. For example, if your individual franchise fee is $35,000, but you are approached by someone who might be persuaded to buy a 10-unit territory and open the units on an accelerated basis, you could offer each unit for $25,000—a $10,000 discount per unit. A customary approach is to take half of the total down ($125,000) and the balance owed on each unit ($12,500) as each units opens. If the franchisee is unable to open each unit on schedule, or if any of the units are in default, then he forfeits the amount paid. The franchisee may continue to operate his existing units, but you now have the right to sell the remainder of the territory to someone else.

As a further incentive to open units promptly, some franchisors discount royalties. In the example cited above, the franchisee would pay the normal six percent royalty for the first unit. But thereafter, the royalty could be discounted by ¼ percent for every two units opened. Upon opening of the third unit, all units would be paying 5¾ percent; with the fifth unit, 5½ percent, and so on. With the opening of the tenth unit, all would be paying five percent. We recommend that franchisors take a very careful look at all factors involved before discounting royalties; they are, after all, your principal source of income. Of course, the cost of supervising one franchise with 10 units will be less than the cost of supervising 10 individual franchises.

If, instead of a multi-unit territory, you are selling the 10-unit territory to a subfranchisor, you might charge $100,000 for the rights to the market and $2,500 for each unit sold. By the time your subfranchisor has sold 10 units, he has collected $350,000, of which you have received $125,000—a 65/35 split of the franchise fees. In this arrangement, you should require that all units be sold within a specified time frame—usually one year. Royalties can be split 60/40, 70/30, or even 80/20, because the subfranchisor is providing nearly all of the necessary supervision and support.

The chart below summarizes examples of franchise fee and royalty payment options for the three types of retail franchise structures:

	Franchise Fees Earned by Franchisor	Royalties Earned by Franchisor
Individual	$35,000	6%
Multi-unit (10 units)	$25,000 each, payable as $125,000 down, $12,500 as each unit opens	6% 1-3 units 5¾% after 3 5½% after 5 5¼% after 7 5% when all 10 open
Sub-franchise	$100,000 for territory plus $2,500 per unit sold	2% (of 6%)

Fee and royalties for conversion franchises vary, but because the franchisor does not provide a full range of services to an existing business, the franchise fee is usually reduced by up to one-half the price of a normal individual franchise, and the royalty sometimes begins at a reduced rate that grows to the franchisor's non-conversion rate after a few years. For example, the rate may start at one percent the first year and increase by a percentage point or two each year until it reaches the full rate the third year. Or it can be determined by using the franchisee's previous year's sales as a ceiling and charging the regular royalty on any sales over that amount.

Other income sources

While royalties are the most important revenue source, there are other income sources for franchisors, including sales of products or services on which the franchisor can make a profit.

Some examples might include products relating to the franchise (such as pet-care products to a pet-grooming salon), or services such as bookkeeping, payroll, or computerized inventory control. But you should approach such avenues of additional revenue with caution, offering a fair price and good value for that price, because abuses relating to the sale of such products and services have led to franchise rebellions and unfavorable (to the franchisor) court decisions. (See Chapter 7.)

Advertising and promotion fees

Advertising fees should not be considered income to the franchisor, and in fact should be administered as trust funds and kept separate from other funds. There usually are two categories of advertising fees:

Local advertising. Franchisees are usually required by the franchise agreement to spend a certain amount—a minimum versus a percentage of sales—on local advertising or promotion programs that the franchisor has approved or developed. Usually, the figure for local advertising is equal to the percentage of sales spent by the franchisor's company-owned unit(s).

Establishing a specific fee at the beginning is essential. If you wait to require this fee until after a number of franchisees have been brought into the system, the original franchisees may decline to participate on the mistaken belief that advertising expenditures build only gross sales (to the benefit of the franchisor), not profits. In effect, then, your early franchisees will get a "free ride" on the backs of later franchisees and you will be powerless to make a change until the terms of their franchise agreements expire.

Corporate advertising. A percentage of sales is deposited in an account administered by the franchisor for the development of advertising materials and concepts. The exact percentage depends upon the nature of your business. Some businesses require no local advertising at all. A client of ours, Value Rent-A-Car, with outlets in or near airports, does not advertise in cities where its outlets are located. Its customers are travelers from other cities and it restricts its advertising to the media of those cities.

Advertising funds have been the subject of numerous disputes by franchisees who felt they were either not spent, or were apportioned inappropriately. We recommend that corporate advertising funds be maintained in accounts separate from the franchisor's other operating accounts, and that the franchisees receive a quarterly report detailing how these monies have been disbursed.

The territory

Almost all good franchise agreements will include language that grants to the franchisee a territory or area of responsibility in which no other franchise or company-owned unit will be situated or conduct business. The principal questions each franchisor must answer regarding territories are: 1. How large should they be? and 2. On what criteria should the size be based?

Criteria can vary widely, depending upon the type of business and especially upon the type of customers catered to by the business. Population alone may be sufficient for a hamburger franchise, but for a computer franchise the number of businesses in a given area may also be important. A travel agency that appeals to people in the upper-middle income bracket may select single family homes as one criterion for a territory. A company that sells electrical equipment to contractors may make contractors of a certain type the sole criterion. Other criteria include the volume of automobile traffic; topographical features such as mountains, rivers, and freeways; and residential or business density.

Even after the criteria for size have been determined, it may not be easy to pinpoint the size itself. One way of approaching that question is to ask another: How large must the territory be to give the franchisee sufficient customers to be profitable? You can begin to answer this question with some accuracy—if you have an existing business—by determining the geographical makeup of your present customer base, perhaps through a survey. If you discover, for example, that three-quarters of the customers of your average unit live within a two-mile radius and that population for the area within two miles of those units averages 20,000 people, you might decide to set your territory size at 25,000 or 30,000 people.

Then, when granting a franchise, it becomes a matter of carving out a geographic territory periodically as the population increases or as other criteria alter.

Territory, by the way, is one aspect of the franchise agreement that can be negotiated without requiring amendments to filings with the states. Generally speaking, however, it is wise to avoid granting territories that are too large. You will have a long time to regret it.

Setting the term

You must have a franchise agreement with your franchisee. But how long should that agreement be in effect? Perpetually? Back in the early days of franchising, franchisors didn't always answer that question intelligently. Tastee-Freez, then a fast-growing chain of ice cream stores, granted a 66-county territory to a franchisee without a performance schedule and with no limit to the duration of the agreement. After 20 years, only nine units were in operation and the franchisee had died. His widow had no desire to open additional units. Tastee Freez was left with two alternatives: 1. Buy back the territory at the franchisee's price, or 2. Allow it to remain undeveloped and lose potential revenues in the millions. Such excruciating decisions can be avoided by establishing a term of agreement and, of course, by not granting a larger territory to any franchisee than he or she can reasonably develop, given your time constraints and the franchisee's financial and operational capabilities.

But what should be the duration of the term? These are the two most important factors to consider:

1. Size of investment. The larger the franchisee's investment, the longer the franchisee will need to recoup it. For example, the term of agreement for a Marriott Inn franchisee is 25 years and for Omni Hotels, Bonanza, and Church's Fried Chicken the term is 15 years. The smallest investment in this group is required by Church's: $359,500 to $700,000. On the other hand, Pier 1 Imports ($100,000) and Baskin-Robbins ($58,747) give five-year agreements. Franchisors will offer even longer terms of agreement to multi-unit buyers, whose investments can range as high as $20 million.

2. Term of the lease. Sometimes, and particularly in enclosed malls, the term of agreement is tied to the lease. When the lease ends, the agreement ends. Typical leases in enclosed malls are three to five years.

In general, we recommend five- to 10-year initial terms, depending upon size of investment, with two or three automatic five-year renewals at the franchisee's option, subject to the franchisee remaining in compliance with the agreement and signing the then-current franchise agreement at the then-current terms. This gives you, the franchisor, the opportunity to revise royalties or other aspects of the agreement periodically. Of course, a franchisee who is in violation of the agreement can be terminated at any time.

Trademarks and logos

Not every franchisable business is blessed with a franchisable name. One of our clients, a retailer of moderately-priced art reproductions and prints, had devised a system for acquiring merchandise at low prices and marketing it profitably to people with widely varying tastes. The simplicity of the business plus its profitability and low cost made it, in our opinion, eminently franchisable. As we do with all our clients, we asked at the beginning of our relationship whether or not he had registered his trademark federally, suspecting at the same time that we knew the answer. No, he had not. Whereupon, after discussions with a specialist in trademark law, he was informed that the likelihood was extremely small that the company's name, Affordable Art, could be registered and protected. We explained that the U.S. Patent and Trademark Office regards names that are nothing more than descriptions of a business as community property, so to speak, and not exclusive. The purpose of obtaining a trademark, of course, is to prevent anyone else throughout the United States from doing business under that name and with that trademark.

Joel Merkur, president of Affordable Art, agreed immediately to search for a new name—never an easy task for a business that likes its name and has been successful with it. And, indeed, the name they chose deviated as little as possible from the original. "Gallery One Affordable Art" was registered federally and the client within a year had sold six individual franchises and a 24-unit territory. Fortunately, at the time the new name was selected, Affordable Art consisted only of five company-owned units, and the cost of changing sign faces and printed materials was negligible.

A trademark is vitally important because it is the symbol of your franchise and conveys to the public that a uniform standard of operation exists in any business bearing that trademark. To be protected nationally, your mark must be registered with the U.S. Patent and Trademark Office, although there are reasons why you may wish to have your mark registered in certain states as well. (One is that after applying for a federal trademark you can expect to wait nearly a year for approval; state registrations are quicker and enable you to establish a record of doing business under that name on a given date, which can be helpful if a conflict arises over the use of the name or mark.)

When seeking to obtain a trademark, it is wise to consult an attorney who specializes in trademark law. The attorney's first step is to conduct a trademark search to determine whether your mark might be the same as or "confusingly similar" to other registered marks already in use elsewhere in the country. The attorney will also explain the requirements and restrictions governing the use of your trademark and will discuss the differences between what attorneys regard as "strong" and "weak" marks. Descriptiveness, as in the case of Affordable Art, is one attribute of a weak mark. Another is the use of surnames, such as Dutton or Jones or Baker. A Mr. McDonald found that he couldn't use his own name when he opened a hamburger restaurant and tried to call it, naturally, McDonald's! The best marks, say the attorneys, are invented words like Exxon, Allegis, and Unisys that in themselves mean nothing and that no business owner in his right mind would adopt without having the substantial assets needed to force acceptance in the marketplace through repetition.

In selecting the name, you should have an eye to the future to avoid picking a name that might limit the direction your business could take. "Kentucky Fried Chicken" certainly implies that they sell chicken, but, at one point in its history, that franchise found it rather difficult to convince the public that it also sold ribs. If you're contemplating entering business or franchising at some future date and you have a name or trademark you would like to register now, to protect and register it you'll find that you must actually use the trademark in interstate commerce; two years of nonuse will leave it subject to abandonment.

The trademark is just one of several items that professionalize your public image. Another very important image-enhancer is a business' logo. A good one will convey in a glance what your business is about and can help attract the kind of customer you desire. A bad one will reflect mediocrity, no matter how excellent all other aspects of your business may be.

Few expenditures you make in the course of your business career will have the lasting value of the dollars you pay a skilled professional designer to create a logo that is forceful, dynamic, subtle, distinguished, playful, sincere, trendy, or whatever other idea is appropriate to your particular business.

Nor should a professional image be limited to your logo—especially if you seek to attract customers to your premises. You can, of course, hire a specialist who will design your entire business structure, including fixtures and signs, in a way that can be readily copied by your franchisees. Other firms will go even farther than that. Royal Store Fixtures, a division of Friel Bernheim (based in Philadelphia), designs the unit and all of the fixtures, and delivers it, prefabricated, then assembles it for a complete turnkey operation. And every one of your franchisees can buy exactly the same product.

Documents and materials

When the business decisions have been made, the next step in the franchise development process is the preparation of various documents and other materials in three areas: legal, operations, and marketing.

Legal documents

We have spoken at length in Chapter 7 about the principal legal documents needed by any franchisor, namely the offering circular and the franchise agrement. We should also mention that separate agreements are required for each type of franchise selected: individual, multi-unit, and subfranchisor. In addition, those documents need to be registered or filed in states that require it. (By the way, registration and filing is not a one-time process, except in the case of Texas. All other states require that each year every franchisor renew its registration annually by filing the latest documents, although the states' fees for renewals are about half the price of the initial filing fee.)

The operations manual

The cornerstone of your franchise program will be your operations manual. If you have built a successful business, you've made mistakes along the way that have probably cost you money, but you don't want your franchisees to make those same mistakes— you want them to replicate your success from the first day on. To ensure that they adopt your business system and adhere to it, you should describe clearly and in detail how that system operates from the moment the business opens each day until it closes. That is the function of the operations manual. Your manual should be divided into sections for easy reference, with pages numbered and perhaps held together in some loose-leaf manner to allow additions as they become necessary.

Each franchisee should sign a receipt for each manual, because the manual not only prescribes your system, it contains your trade secrets and is lent to the franchisee during the term of the agreement. It always remains the property of the franchisor. Finally, it should be noted that the manual, even to a greater degree than the franchise agreement, sets forth the standards for your business that the franchisee is expected to meet. Without an operations manual, a franchisee can always claim, "They never told me that." With it, you can respond by citing chapter and page.

We've prepared a suggested outline for a sample operations manual for a retail outlet, to show just how detailed and comprehensive such a manual must be:

Operations Manual Outline

ABC Franchise Systems, Inc.
A. INTRODUCTION
   Letter from the President
   Instructions for using this manual
   Notice of policy/procedure change
   Suggested change of procedure
   Your franchise agreement
   The ABC Franchise Systems, Inc. philosophy
   Responsibilities of an ABC franchisee
B. FRANCHISE ORGANIZATION
   History of ABC Franchise Systems, Inc.
   ABC Franchise Systems, Inc. organizational structure
   President
   Director of Franchising
   Controller
   Director of Marketing and Sales
   Director of Franchise Operations
   Director of Training
   Director of Advertising
   Organizational Chart
   Services of ABC Franchise Systems, Inc.
   Franchise Relations
C. PRE-OPENING PROCEDURES
   Introduction
   Selecting your business type

Selecting professional advisors
Pre-opening checklist
Site selection
Negotiating your lease
Leasehold improvements
Layout and design specifications
Recommended equipment and supplies
Sample opening inventory
  Approved vendors/brands
Indoor and outdoor signage
Licenses and permits
Utilities and services
Insurance
Banking relations and services
Taxes
Office filing system
Franchisee training program
D. MANAGEMENT
Introduction
Basic management
Your function as owner/manager
Generating profit
Time management
Stress management
ABC Franchise Systems, Inc. reporting policies
  Sales reports
  Sample ABC profit and loss statement
  Sample ABC balance sheet
E. PERSONNEL
Policy on EEO and Affirmative Action
Fair Employment Practices
  Pre-employment inquiries
  Wage and hour law
Staff selection
The manager you hire

Job descriptions
  Manager
  Assistant manager
  Salesperson
The employment process
  Sample ads
  Application for employment with ABC
  Authorization to release information
  Reference letter—previous employer
  Telephone reference check
Interview guidelines
  Sample interview questions
Orientation of employees
  Orientation checklist
Employee records
Scheduling
ABC personnel policies
Evaluating the sales staff
  ABC employee review
Probationary status
  Employee counseling
Dismissing employees
  Resignation
  Termination
ABC employee handbook
F. DAILY STORE OPERATIONAL PROCEDURES
  Introduction
  Recommended store hours
  Daily opening and closing procedures
  Money handling
    Cash register procedures
    Daily sales report
    Change funds
    Petty cash
  Accepting payment
    Cash payments

Check acceptance procedures
Guidelines for acceptance procedures
Credit card procedures
Payment with a gift certificate
Layaway payment procedures
  Merchandise credit procedures
Tax exempt sales
Gift certificate sales
Merchandise returns, refunds, exchanges
Emergency/security procedures
Inventory
Approved vendors
  Vendor relations
Purchasing
  Selecting merchandise
  Using the purchase order
Receiving
Pricing
  Proper ticketing procedures
  Markdowns
Damaged/defective merchandise
Vendor returns
  Documentation letters
Transfers
Store administration
The merchandise budget process
Visits from headquarters
  ABC store survey form
G. SALES & MERCHANDISING
Customer service
  Handling customer complaints
  Proper telephone etiquette
Sales
  Product knowledge
  Greeting the customer
  Qualifying the customer

Add-on selling techniques
Closing
Merchandise display guidelines
Sample display plan
Special services
Special orders
Donations
H. ADVERTISING
Advertising requirements
ABC Franchise System, Inc.'s advertising philosophy
Methods of advertising
Ordering advertising materials
Approval and placement of advertising
Regional advertising promotions
Special promotions
Planning and scheduling
Community relations
Sample advertising
The grand opening
Suggested grand opening themes or event ideas
I. RECORD KEEPING AND ACCOUNTING
Introduction
Internal controls
Basic accounting equation
Cash vs. accrual basis
Original record of transactions
Books of original entry
Petty cash vouchers
Chart of accounts
Chart of accounts (figure)
Mini chart of accounts (figure)
Balance sheet accounts—detailed description
Income statement accounts—detailed description
Monthly and annual closing procedures
Depreciation guidelines
Multi-unit accounting

Cost accounting guidelines
Operating ratios
Budgeting techniques
  Estimated cash forecast (figure)
Financial planning
  Sample income and expense statement
  Break-even chart (figure)
Financial statement analysis

Some franchise companies also include a toll-free telephone number in their operations manuals so that franchisees can get quick answers to their questions.

Related to the operations manual are the establishment of the franchisor's corporate operational structure, and the systems and forms the franchisees will use. The analysis of the corporate operational structure should spell out the responsibilities, objectives, and duties of each department or division of the franchisor. This analysis can assist the initial and future growth of both the franchisor and the franchise program. Also crucial to this ongoing development are business systems and forms that are easy to use for the franchise and informative for the franchisor. These monitoring and reporting devices should track sales, personnel, research, support, and other areas relevant to the particular franchise program.

Training

One of the most important operational steps is the establishment and overseeing of a useful and meaningful training program. The training program is your first opportunity to spend any significant time with your franchisees, and vice versa. This is the time when they not only learn your system, but also decide whether they've made the right choice in buying your franchise—and you decide whether you've sold to the right candidates.

If your new franchisees fail to successfully complete the training program, or evidence such unhappiness with the system that it appears unlikely they'll succeed, now is the time to terminate the agreement and, if necessary, refund a portion of their franchise fees. The long-term success of your franchise program depends upon the willingness and ability of the franchisees to make it work.

Training facilities vary according to the type of business being franchised, but certainly an operating prototype will be the primary training center, since franchisees need hands-on, on-the-job experience in actual day-to-day operations.

Supplementary training can be given in a classroom. It's not necessary that you build an elaborate headquarters to train your franchisees in the beginning, but you should be able to communicate to them that they are joining a professionally-managed, well-executed operation that expects the highest quality standards to be upheld.

A formal training program, with a curriculum and a schedule, plus any supporting materials that would be helpful, should be designed and presented in a businesslike manner. All of the systems and forms that are used in the operation of the franchise should be thoroughly explained, both in the classroom and on the job, so that franchisees understand why they are used. A training period may be as short as a few days, or as long as two years (as in the case of McDonald's), but three to six weeks is normal, after which the franchisor may spend another week or two on-site with the franchisee assisting in the start-up process.

Marketing

Although we will fully cover all of the aspects of marketing a franchise program in the next chapter, the two elements that need to be scheduled for development are the marketing plan and the various collateral materials needed to reinforce this plan.

Your marketing plan should identify the profile of your average prospective franchise buyer, determine how and where to reach this buyer through various marketing strategies, and suggest the sales approach best calculated to appeal to this buyer. The materials to be created to help reach and appeal to this buyer can include franchise ads, videotapes, flyers, direct-mail pieces, question-and-answer sheets, and—most importantly—your franchise brochure. The brochure should be a professionally produced, full-color piece that presents the story of your franchise program and its advantages to investors. The brochure should also spell out some preliminary facts about your franchise, such as general costs and operational qualifications of the franchisee.

Getting it done

The franchise development process, incorporating all of the activities we have mentioned in this chapter and involving simultaneous activity and proper coordination of the various disciplines involved, is likely to require four to six months. Done piecemeal, of course, the process can take a good deal longer. When it is completed, you will be ready to sell franchises. Your next question may be: How does all this get done and what does it cost? Let's take these questions one at a time.

Unless you and your staff happen to have an extraordinary diversity of skills and experience in franchising, plus a great deal of time, it's safe to say you'll need professional help putting your franchise development program together. You may even want an expert opinion as to the franchisability of your business before committing to what will be, unquestionably, a significant expenditure. Essentially, then, you will have two alternatives: 1. You can hire specialists at each stage of the development process: an attorney for the legal documents, an advertising agency for the marketing materials, a technical writer for the operations manual, specialists to assist in training, financial experts to help you plan your capital formation needs and guide you and your franchises to the right sources of finance, and senior level franchise executives available for consultation during the first year; or 2. You can retain an experienced franchise consulting firm that will undertake all of these activites, preferably under the same roof.

The problem with hiring individual specialists is that you can pay a great deal of money without any guarantee that the individual entities will work together. You may discover at the end, for example, that the franchise agreement and operations manual do not relate to one another as they should; or that the marketing materials were neither written with franchise law in mind nor checked with your attorney; or that your business needs as they relate to franchising were not communicated to your attorney and thus they were not properly expressed in your franchise agreement. There can be problems as well with engaging a franchise consultant, especially the sole practitioner who promises to "consult" with you and "coordinate" the work of others not on his staff.

On the other hand, the right franchise consulting firm can give you the information you need to make an intelligent decision on franchising and also perform all of the tasks required for franchise development using on-staff professionals. An experienced consulting firm capable of performing all of the franchise development services under one roof gives you the added assurance that each task will be coordinated with the other, a factor of considerable importance when critical legal issues are involved. The result for you can be a considerable saving of money, but, equally important, a saving of both your time individually and the time needed to get the job done.

The best approach to finding the help you need is to investigate carefully. One source of assistance is the International Franchise Association (1350 New York Ave., N.W., Suite 900, Washington, DC 20005). They will give you a list of businesses that offer franchise development services. Write for the brochures of these companies. Talk with them on the phone.

Select if you can, companies with a proven track record for assisting successful franchisors. Then narrow your list to one or two and visit their places of business. Be sure to meet their staff and review the quality of work they have completed for other clients that is a matter of public record. Most important, get a list of at least 10 clients of the firms you investigate and call them.

Paying for it

The cost of becoming a franchisor can be divided into two parts. One part consists of the basic services and documents we have described in this chapter that are essential to the creation of a franchise program and the sale of franchises. We call it the franchise development program, and we believe a fair price ranges between $50,000 and $150,000. (Of course, you can pay a great deal more and someone may even offer to do it for less.) Why such a wide range? One variable is whether or not you want to sell multi-unit or subfranchise territories in addition to individual units. If so, you may need three sets of legal documents and marketing materials instead of one. For a subfranchisor, you'll also need a separate operating manual. Another variable is your present cash position. If you need to finance your franchise development program, you may want a business plan to help interest investors. Do you need a franchise sales videotape or a site-selection manual? If you do, the price goes up.

Once your franchise development program is in place, you have the choice of moving ahead at whatever pace suits your goals and your budget. It is possible for a new franchisor to use the less expensive lead-generating methods we will enumerate in Chapter 9 and to bring the first franchisees on board at relatively little cost. Or, the franchisor can launch an expensive national advertising publicity campaign to sell franchises. Between these extremes are many options. Just remember, if you do intend to sell large numbers of franchises quickly, be ready to put in place the personnel you need to train and service your franchisees.

As important as money is to any expansion program, it should not be the most important factor in determining whether or not you should franchise your business. More important are the answers to three other questions: 1. Do I believe in the growth potential of my business? 2. Can franchising give me an edge over my competitors? And 3. Have I the right temperament to be a franchisor?

If the answer to these questions is "yes," franchising would appear to be the next step. But to successfully build a franchise program you must generate leads and sell franchises. That is the focus of the next chapter.

Going To Market

"If a man builds a better mousetrap than his neighbor, the world will beat a path to his door," is an oft-quoted observation of 19th century philosopher Ralph Waldo Emerson. That may have been true in the slower-paced world of Emerson's time, but in today's sophisticated marketplace, you can't wait around for the world to discover you and your new idea. Today, the world needs to know where to find you, wants to see if indeed your "trap" can catch mice, and then compares it with the "better mousetrap" your neighbor is selling. Thus it is with franchising. You may have a brilliant business concept and you may have developed a program to make your concept eminently franchisable, but before you can achieve your goal of expansion via a chain of successful franchises, you must be able to take that concept to market—to deliver it, in an enticing form, to potential franchisees.

The process of marketing a franchise program can be broken down to four steps: 1. Planning; 2. Generating leads of potential franchisees; 3. Following up leads; and 4. Selling franchises. Each of these steps includes a number of important points and considerations. This chapter is divided into four sections to separately cover each step.

Planning

According to a 1987 poll conducted by The Roper Organization for *The Wall Street Journal*, 91 percent of Americans see being able to own their own businesses as an essential part of the "American Dream." Clearly, you do not need to look far to find plenty of people pre-sold on business ownership. And franchising is gaining more and more acceptance as *the* way to get into business for yourself. The aim of your franchise marketing plan is to attract qualified members of the interested public and then persuade them to invest in *your* particular franchise.

Toward this end, we recommend that you prepare—or have prepared—a franchise marketing plan that incorporates the answers—for your specific franchise—to marketing questions we will discuss throughout this chapter. The plan will enable you to decide in advance the direction your marketing program should take, the way it should be structured, and its cost.

Who are your target franchisees?

The first question to be addressed in your marketing plan is, "Who are my principal franchise prospects?" You may be tempted to respond, "Anyone who can afford to buy one"—especially if the pressure to recover your investment in your franchise program is growing. But the fact is—and we cannot emphasize it strongly enough—that nothing you will do before or after will be as important as the selection and support of your first ten (or so) franchisees. If these franchises succeed, your program will have taken a giant step forward. But if they have failed, or you have not provided the services you promised, the consequences to your franchise program can be very grave indeed. And you can be sure that the success or failure of your franchisees will become known. The law requires you to list in your disclosure document the names and addresses of your franchisees, and they will be the first people a perceptive franchisee prospect will call to determine the success of your program. Moreover, the fact is that although the franchisor can only legally make very generalized earnings claims in most states, no law prevents a franchisee from replying about his own experiences to a prospect who asks, "How much can I make in this business?" Satisfied franchisees can become your best salespeople. But remember—the best franchise salesperson in the world cannot overcome negative comments by franchisees.

Who, then, are your most desirable franchise prospects, and how do you get your story across to them? Before addressing either question, we would like to make two important points related to the concept of target groups:

1. Unless you are offering a conversion franchise of a specific existing business, there is no such thing as a "typical" franchise buyer—not in general and not for any particular franchise. There are *many* potential buyers for any given franchise concept. These potential franchisees may share a number of characteristics, but each comes from a unique background, and should be regarded accordingly. While it may be helpful to determine an average or norm for potential franchisees (to help you decide where and how your marketing efforts might have their best effect), these targets should not be used as be-all and end-all yardsticks against which to measure potential franchisees.

2. As your franchise program evolves and your chain of franchised units grows, your pool of potential franchisees will probably change characteristics—perhaps radically so, creating a situation where you should be marketing your program to an entirely different target group. This can be caused by changes in price (an increase in fees and/or royalties), region (because of economic or sociological differences from previ-

ous areas), or image (for example, Copy Mat is a franchise that increased its appeal to potential franchisees *and* customers by upgrading the general perception of copy shops). It may also have to do with the objectives of the program. As we have mentioned elsewhere, Burger King—in the early stages of its development—sold subfranchise rights for New Orleans and Chicago, thereby obtaining large cash payments helpful to its expansion program, as well as important market penetration. Later, the company discontinued subfranchising entirely and bought back both the Chicago and New Orleans territories. You must be able to alter your franchisee profile to fit the market and your own needs, and then act to modify your marketing approach accordingly.

Types of franchisees

Franchising has become quite sophisticated since its "growing pains" period of the 1960s, and today it attracts knowledgeable franchisors whose franchise programs are usually the result of both good business practices and sound legal advice. Not only does this make for a more competitive franchise sales environment, it also attracts a better-informed group of prospective franchisees, ranging from former corporate executives with time and money to invest to large corporations buying extensive franchise territories.

In general, good franchisees are rule-followers. To draw a musical analogy, they are the people who, if given the sheet music, could play a beautiful melody. But if they were confronted with a piano and no music, they would find it hard to improvise. That's not to say that they are not bright, but their talent is for implementation, not innovation. In other words, franchisees should be managers, responsible for the general operation of the unit, for management of the staff, and for working effectively with suppliers. Franchisees should also have sales ability, because, when you get right down to it, no business exists unless somebody sells something. Franchisees generally are people who will be dealing with the public much of the time, and they should be able to sell your product or service to those consumers. They should be enthusiastic about the franchise, and capable of communicating that enthusiasm to their employees and customers.

In recent years, there has been an increasing trend of large companies becoming franchisees—especially by purchasing and developing sizable territories. Some of these companies own franchises of more than one franchisor and have become public companies. Despite this growing trend, the backbone of franchising is still (and will remain, we believe) the individual owner/operator. These are the franchisees (unless otherwise noted) we will be primarily discussing in this section.

Keeping in mind that generalities and stereotypes can be, at best, useful shorthand, what follows are identifications of and discussions about some of the more common types of franchisees.

Business professionals/middle managers

Today's era of the all-pervasive MBA, the weeding-out of middle management, and corporate mergers and takeovers has created a glut of "outplaced" or early-retired managers and other businesspeople. *The New York Times* estimated that more than 12 million white collar jobs were eliminated in 1986. In many cases, these people are looking for new business challenges and the chance to be their own bosses. Businesspeople who have become accustomed to the protective custody of a corporation may find the risk of starting businesses entirely on their own too formidable. To them the independence-with-a-safety-net of a franchise can be very appealing.

These middle managers and other professionals have become sought-after as potential franchisees for a number of reasons: they already understand the nature of productive teamwork and rule-following; they have the financial means, from savings and from severance benefits, to become franchisees; and they can bring general business acumen, experience, and entrepreneurial drive to a franchise. Often, these franchisees are the best candidates—

once they've proven successful—for additional franchise outlets.

The major drawbacks with this type of franchisee can include: *too much* entrepreneurial drive (great in franchisors, but potentially counterproductive in franchisees); entrenched ways of doing business that may be opposed to your system; and a habit of relying upon a cadre of support personnel that many corporate managers take for granted.

"Mom-and-pops"

So-called because of their similarity to the neighborhood couples who owned corner groceries years ago, "mom-and-pops" are couples who run franchise outlets. Today's mom-and-pop franchisees can be "yuppie" couples, immigrant families eager to be their own bosses, or retirees investing their nest eggs and golden years. Mom-and-pop franchisees can have advantages, but they also carry some very definite drawbacks. On the plus side: most mom-and-pop franchisees are used to working for someone, and usually find it easy and natural to follow a franchisor's lead; they usually come into a particular franchise without experience in that type of business, and therefore without preconceived notions of how the business should be run; and, after investing their savings and futures in the outlet, mom-and-pops are likely to work long and hard to make the business work.

The mom-and-pop prospects may be the quickest to respond to your franchise marketing program and first to buy, but the lack of sophistication that makes them relatively easy sales in the first place could work against you in the long run in terms of poor unit performance and reduced royalties. In addition, they will probably require—at least in the early stages—a great deal of supervision. They may also have a low amount of ready savings and/or available financing. While that last drawback can be the hardest to overcome, couples often have a better chance at getting financing than they might realize: It is estimated that the *average* homeowner has $30,000 available in home equity.

Absentee investors

Assume you are a franchisor requiring a financial commitment of more than $1 million per unit from your franchisees. At that price, the profile you seek is obviously not the mom-and-pop or manager type. Instead, you need an investor type. While business-format franchising has grown primarily on the strength and commitment of owner/operators (and will continue to do so, as we predicted earlier), many franchises have been built successfully through sales to investors. Some franchises that do not—as a policy—sell franchises to absentee owners or investors *do* solicit investors to purchase real estate or other major assets, such as specialized and/or expensive equipment, for the franchisee. The investor then leases the real estate or equipment to the people who run the business on a daily basis.

One franchisor that utilizes investors in this way is Schlotzsky's, an Austin, Texas-based deli/bakery franchise. Schlotzsky's is actually a co-general partner with a management company that raises funds from passive investors. Schlotzsky's then hires a management staff to operate the units under the supervision of the franchisor. The Marriott Corporation works in a similar fashion. Marriott sells the hotel real estate to one investor group and the franchise to another. Then Marriott comes in and actually manages the hotel on behalf of the franchisee, charging a management fee plus an incentive fee based on profits. We believe that this trend towards innovative and complex relationships between franchisors, management groups, franchisees, and investors will continue to allow businesses to expand through franchising in ways that would otherwise not be possible.

Employees and customers

The people who are most familiar with your business—your employees (especially store managers), your customers, and even your suppliers—can be an important source of franchisees. In fact, many of our franchisor clients have admitted to being awakened to the potential of franchising by customers and other daily contacts who began asking if franchises were available.

The primary advantage of franchisees from this group is that they know your business and are already enthusiastic supporters of it. If the prospects are qualified, these can be the easiest franchise sales you will ever make. The major downside is financial. Many people who inquire about franchises have no idea about their cost. And the average store manager—unless he or she has retired after a long career elsewhere—may not have the financial ability to become a franchisee. One way around this problem is to adopt in-house financing programs similar to those offered by Domino's Pizza and Bubba's Breakaway (among others). In some cases, the franchisor offers financing to employees who have reached a certain rank or level of seniority. In other cases, the franchisor refers potential franchisees to a particular bank or finance group that is supportive of their business and franchise program. (Franchisor and franchisee financing options are more fully discussed in Chapter 11.)

Conversion, multi-unit, and subfranchisors

One of the principal advantages of a conversion franchise program is ease of targeting the franchisee. Whether your prospective franchisee is a real estate broker, a hotel operator, a dentist, or the owner of whatever business you wish to convert to a franchise outlet, the question is not, "How do I find such people in order to get my message across to them?" The question is, "How do I persuade them that I have something to offer that will improve their business enough to justify the franchise fee and royalty I'm asking for?" That question is best answered by companies that franchise in fragmented industries where a strong marketing presence has not yet been established on a national basis by any single competitor. To be successful the franchisor must launch a powerful campaign that enlists people who are concerned for their future or who want some means of obtaining an edge over the competition. Comprehensive Accounting, for example, gives accountants who are struggling or new to the business world a proven business system as well as the traditional advantages of conversion franchising: a unified name and marketing program. Re/Max Realty gives real estate agents a way to retain their full commissions; they share office and advertising costs rather than work as employees for brokers.

Multi-unit franchisees tend to be similar to individual franchisees—except they have more money. More and more large corporations are also moving into multi-unit franchising. Examples of these include Greyhound Food Management, Inc., one of the largest Burger King franchisees; Po Folks, a franchisor of Po Folks Restaurants, but also a Wendy's franchisee; Collins Food International, a large Kentucky Fried Chicken franchisee and 70 percent owner of Sizzler Steak Houses; and Calney Foods, the largest Taco Bell franchisee. All of these companies actually own and operate franchises in multiple-unit territories.

Generally, subfranchisors are quite different from individual and multi-unit franchisees. They usually are experienced businesspeople with heavy sales backgrounds and substantial financial resources. Marketing for subfranchisors will require a separate and distinct campaign—usually more sophisicated than a campaign for individual franchisees.

Where will your franchises be located?

Having determined—to the extent possible—the profile of your franchisee, your next marketing decision concerns where to establish early franchises. In general, we recommend launching your franchise program in one distinct region—ideally, a region located close to your prototype business or company headquarters. As a simple matter of geography, this tactic helps conserve your financial and personnel resources while getting the first few franchises up and running. You need to be close enough to identify and respond to problems quickly. You must tend these first franchises carefully, because, as we have pointed out, they will be invaluable promoters of your franchise program.

Another reason for starting out locally is that the first franchise buyers are likely to be people who are already familiar with your business—your customers, suppliers, or employees. By opening other units in the same area, they can capitalize on your name and reputation, as well as the advantages of cooperative advertising and perhaps even cooperative buying. One of our clients, Big Ed's, a franchisor of hamburger restaurants, expanded through franchising from three to 26 units without getting out of the state of Oklahoma. There, contented with the size of his company, Ed Thomas, owner of Big Ed's, stopped his expansion program.

We have seen several franchisors attempt to bypass this relatively slow but effective process. One launched a national program to sell franchises, complete with a full-blown national closed-circuit television presentation to business brokers who were expected to sell franchises, even before the prototype unit was profitable. (Only later did the franchisor learn it *wouldn't* be.) Others have advertised widely and received numerous sales leads that they were not prepared to follow up. Usually these franchisors exhaust their financial resources before their program has the time to become successful. But where capital is sufficient and the concept intriguing enough, a national rollout can succeed. Video's 1st, a franchisor of video-rental kiosks designed for shopping center parking lots, launched a franchise advertising campaign nationally in *The Wall Street Journal* and within two months had sold 110 franchises.

Generating leads

No franchise program gets very far without prospective franchisees. As a franchisor-to-be you may have had people inquire about whether or not you are going to franchise. In fact, as we have said, many of our clients are motivated to franchise by people who visit their places of business and tell them, "If you ever decide to franchise, let me know." The best response to this is to take the names and addresses of such people and say, "I'm planning to franchise, but I can't talk to you about our program yet. As soon as I can do so legally, I'll get back in touch with you." Almost all franchisors have access to such leads. Some, when properly cultivated, may turn into franchise sales. Beefy's, the double drive-thru hamburger franchise from Nashville, sold its first dozen or so franchises to people who saw long lines of cars at the units and didn't need an ad to point out the potential. Most leads of this kind, however, will not be converted into franchise sales. So the question is, once all of the other aspects of your franchise program are in place, how will you generate franchise sales leads?

Networking

The easiest way to begin spreading the word about your franchise program is through indirect methods, such as networking and posting in-store notices. These methods can help generate interest in your program while you gear up for more focused— and more expensive—means of generating leads.

Networking gets the word out to people who know you, and to people who know them. Tell your professional business contacts—such as salespeople, suppliers, bankers, etc.—that you are looking for qualified franchisees. (Better yet, write them a letter.) Ask these contacts to mention your program to friends and associates who might be interested. Or take recommendations from them and then contact these people yourself. Your goal is to position your program in people's minds. People need to know that you are selling franchises and what your franchises consist of, and your professional contacts can greatly assist with this task.

As we mentioned earlier in this chapter, another important source of leads is your customers. By simply posting a professional-looking sign in your outlets that reads, "Franchises available—call for information," you can tap into a group of people who already support your business, some of whom may be very interested in buying a franchise. Posting sign-up sheets for mailing lists can also be a useful technique to generate leads at the store level.

Of course, don't overlook your existing consumer advertising. A small notice at the bottom of display ads or a brief mention in radio or television commercials that franchises are available will cost nothing extra. It should be noted, however, that relatively untargeted methods such as these can be relatively ineffective as well.

Public relations

In response to a recent survey, a group of our most successful franchisor clients ranked franchisee referrals and publicity as their two most important sources of franchise leads. As a new franchisor, you will not enjoy franchisees referrals at first; but you would do well to put public relations at or near the top of your franchise marketing program.

Why does publicity carry such power? As we have indicated throughout this book, we believe that nothing is more important to the sale of a franchise than credibility. Mentions of your franchise program in the news or features pages of newspapers and magazines, or interviews with you on radio or television can go a long way toward establishing your credibility with prospective franchisees. In the public mind, anyone who can afford it can put an ad in the paper, but only the "deserving" are the subject of a news or feature article.

Of course, the truth is somewhat less definite. Certainly, publicity cannot be "bought" in the direct sense, but it is also true that it is rarely obtained free of charge or effort. Sure, you can call the editor of your local newspaper and tell him that you are franchising. If your city isn't too large and it's a slow news day, maybe he'll send somebody to write a story about it. But after that, what then? The answer should be a well-rounded public relations program conducted by professionals who know what editors, writers, and producers want in the way of a story, and who know how to keep after them until the story is printed or broadcast.

Franchise advertising

While publicity can be very useful, it should not be solely relied upon to generate leads. You will need a steady stream of franchise leads to maintain the growth of your program. As we have indicated, many new franchisors advertise in local markets—generally using newspapers—before advancing to regional or national publications. If you choose this method, you should determine in your marketing plan which individual markets are best for your franchise program, and which publications in those markets are best for reaching your target audience. Criteria for markets can include such factors as household income, number of single-family homes, number of businesses of a given type, or other statistics related to the customer base for your particular business. Circulation will be one criterion for the publications you choose, but others can be income level of readership and popularity of the business sections. On a regional level, we have already mentioned the Thursday *Wall Street Journal's* Mart Section as an excellent forum for franchise ads. When you are ready to advertise nationally, you should consider, in particular, publications such as *Venture, Inc.*, and *Entrepreneur*. Of these publications, we would especially recommend *Venture* to franchisors seeking relatively affluent franchisees, either for individual or multi-unit sales.

Few franchisors use radio, television, or billboards to advertise for franchise sales. Costs are prohibitive and the audience of these media is too diverse for a narrowly focused franchise sales message. For a time, programs on cable television sought to attract franchisor advertisers by focusing specifically on franchise opportunities, but one by one these programs left the air. However, at least one franchisor we know of—Stained Glass Overlay—has had some success with commercials on cable television.

Seminars and open houses

The immediate goal of most franchise ads is to generate a phone call or letter, which will lead, in turn, to a face-to-face interview. Another option—particularly if your concept is either distinctive or complex—is to invite the public to attend a "free seminar featuring a new and exciting franchise opportunity." Respondents to the ad will probably recognize that the "seminar" is really a sales presentation, but it allows them to avoid the pressure of a one-on-one sales situation while obtaining information they require to make a decision. If you or someone on your staff has strong speaking skills, a seminar might be worth considering. At least one franchisor, Subway (submarine-sandwich shops), uses this technique frequently.

The open house is another way of easing the prospect into a sales situation. Pick a time when your store is at least moderately busy and invite people interested in owning their own businesses to see yours in action. You can use both networking and advertising to attract interested prospects.

Shows

Another way of generating leads is to attend business opportunity and franchise shows, or, if appropriate, trade shows. Business opportunity shows are held throughout the country, usually on weekends at downtown or airport hotels. Many of these shows feature low-cost and, to some degree, suspect businesses. However, the franchise opportunity shows, including those sponsored by the International Franchise Association, are generally more professional. Franchisors who attend these shows should be prepared to provide hand-outs and, if possible, show a videotaped presentation.

Copy and layout

Creating a good franchise ad is an art in itself. Your market is very specialized, consisting primarily of people who happen to be looking for a business opportunity at the moment your ad appears. Your "product" is very expensive, in terms of both the buyer's time and commitment. And it's a complex product—one that took at least four to eight pages to describe in your franchise brochure (more about the brochure later in this chapter). How do you develop a franchise ad that offers information about your business and appeals to the audience you're after?

"Big name" franchisors usually stress their track record: "More than 800 franchises sold;" "30 percent of our franchisees buy a second unit within six months." At the beginning, of course, you can't use that approach. So you'll want to concentrate on articulating the most important advantage your business offers. Perhaps you have a unique way to appeal to a well-recognized market. Or perhaps your business requires an unusually low investment. You don't need to tell the whole story—just convey enough of the appeal of your franchise to make the reader want to learn more.

Sometimes a picture really can be worth a thousand words. For example, our client, Video's 1st, whom we mentioned earlier, received more than 300 inquiries from an ad they placed in *The Wall Street Journal*, which depicted their unit with just a few words emphasizing the market potential of the concept: "What a great idea! A drive-up video rental franchise!" Other franchises may require more detailed copy, but you should always try to keep it as simple, straightforward, and attention-getting as you can.

Here are some other benefit-oriented franchise ad headlines from the *Journal*:

Isn't it time you made some serious money?
—Prescott Forbes Group
Start out with 60 years experience.
—Tinder Box International
If you'll never be president of the company you're with, maybe you need a new company. YOUR OWN.
—VR Business Brokers
Be a service leader to the medical industry.
—Deliverex
Keep America working and get paid for it!
—Snelling and Snelling, Inc.

"Why I wanted to be a consultant."
—General Business Services, Inc.

The profile of your franchisee—and your decisions as to where and how fast you want to sell—will help determine what sort of ad you want to run. For example, if you are seeking owner/operators of a low-investment business, and want to confine your franchise sales for the moment to a specific city (or cities), you may find a modest-sized ad in the local newspaper's business opportunity classified section to be cost-effective. Such an ad will probably be all copy (no illustrations) and relatively short. On the other hand, if you need a franchisee with heavier capital requirements, you should consider a larger ad in the financial pages. Your copy, in this case, may address a more sophisticated investor and give more details—although you should be careful not to tell too much. Or you might appeal to a specific background or life situation, pitching your appeal to individuals with sales experience or to displaced middle managers, for example.

Cost per lead, cost per franchisee

How do you determine the effectiveness of your advertising? The simple answer, of course, is that effective ads bring in leads that are converted into franchisees. However, that can be too simplistic. The advertising can be doing its job, but, for one reason or another, your program may not be attracting the right people or your sales program may not be adequate. To better evaluate franchise advertising, you should focus on the number of leads it generates and the quality of each lead. As a rule of thumb, we tell our clients to expect to pay $30 to $100 in advertising expense for each qualified lead. What is a qualified lead? Someone who has the financial ability—although not necessarily the desire—to buy a franchise. (More about qualifying leads later in this chapter.) It is the task of the lead follow-up program and the sales program to transform a qualified lead into a franchisee.

Now you have gotten the word out on your franchise program, and are beginning to receive inquiries from interested parties.

The next step of your marketing program is to follow up these leads, focusing on turning these inquiries into sales and the interested parties into franchisees.

Lead follow-up

Our recommendation when a lead is received—whether it is from a referral by a franchisee (or other individual) or from the response to an ad—is that, to save your sales staff's valuable time, a secretary should take the person's name, address, and telephone number and simply say, "I would like to send you some information about our franchise program. After you receive the material, our franchise director will call to answer any questions you may have." At the same time, the secretary should find out exactly (if possible) when, where, and how the candidate found out about your program (to track the effectiveness of the different segments of your marketing efforts). When the call is concluded, a franchise brochure should be immediately sent to the prospect.

The franchise brochure

We pointed out earlier that as a franchisor, you are embracing an entirely new business. No longer will you be solely in the pizza, car wash, plant care, or whatever business you are now in—you will also be in the franchise business. So it follows that your advertising and promotional efforts will no longer be used only to sell pizzas, car washes, plant care, etc. You will need new materials, specially designed to follow up your leads and set the sales process in motion.

The most basic and generally most important piece of promotional material you will employ is the franchise brochure. Because, especially for the new franchisor, it will often create that critically important first impression, the brochure must appear as professional and appealing as possible. An attractive, well-written brochure not only enables the person inquiring to determine whether or not he or she wants to pursue the matter further, it also permits others connected with the prospect to share that information. Buying a franchise represents a major financial and career decision for most people. The spouse, relatives, attorney, accountant, and banker of the prospect all may become involved in the decision, and your franchise brochure may, indeed, be closely examined by all of them.

A brochure designed to explain and promote a franchise is, by its nature, more complicated than most brochures written to describe a product or service. Of course (and this applies to all of your franchise advertising), it must conform to the state laws that govern franchise sales advertising. Because several states scrutinize franchise sales ads with almost as much intensity as they do franchise legal documents, the regulatory agencies of those states will routinely prohibit, among other things, earnings claims for company-owned units, earnings claims for franchisees (unless previously filed with the state), and promises of profitability and success in general. In addition, state agencies have been known to ask for verification of any statistics given in a franchise brochure. Moreover, the content of the brochure must be consistent with the content of your legal documents, even though the language will be quite different. If you prepare a brochure specifically for use in states that do not regulate franchise sales, and later choose to expand your program into states that *do* require registration, you may be forced to reprint the brochure—incorporating the proper language for the registration states.

Aside from legal considerations, a franchise brochure is complex because it really must perform two separate functions. First, it must persuade the reader that whatever product or service the franchise outlets are selling to their customers is attractive, useful, and has a point of difference from that of the competition—if, indeed, that is the case. But by far the most important function of the brochure is to convey to the reader the advantages of your business system. Few connoisseurs of the hamburger would rate a McDonald's burger as the best on the market, yet anyone with a knowledge of business operations recognizes the

McDonald's system—from site selection to franchisee training to store operations to marketing—as one of the finest of its kind. A brochure must clearly distinguish between product or service and business system *and* deal effectively with both to properly serve your franchise sales program.

We are continually astonished how many franchisors—after thoroughly addressing planning, organizational, and legal needs—produce badly-designed, even shoddy franchise brochures. In some cases, presumably, the franchisor has exhausted his funds early or has rushed the brochure to completion for some reason. But it also seems apparent that some franchisors do not place high importance on the brochure, instead assuming that their name and reputation speak for themselves. Whatever the philosophy of large, established franchisors toward franchise brochures, there seems to be no question that a high-quality franchise brochure is essential for the franchisor just entering the marketplace. For the new franchisor, a professionally designed and written four-color brochure is not—in our opinion—a luxury; it is an absolute necessity.

Accordingly, we offer the following important dos and don'ts for preparing a franchise brochure:

THE DOS AND DON'TS OF FRANCHISE BROCHURES

DO...	DON'T...
• Get it printed professionally	• Try to save money at the expense of quality (it will show)
• Use upbeat, professional color photography with people in the pictures	• Use illustrations (makes the business look "proposed") or photos of deserted-looking, empty units
• Give cogent, concise information about the franchise and franchisor	• Tell your life story

- Use an insert or pullout that can be easily replaced to convey information that can become outdated quickly (such as outlet totals and locations)
- Prepare the brochure with your specific audience in mind—it should reflect who your target franchisees are
- Check the legality of information and wording with an experienced franchise attorney
- Use clear charts, graphics, and comparisons to present the growth of your business and/or industry
- Thoughtfully assess the nature of your industry and your business' position in it

- Make your brochure an "action document" designed to encourage personal interviews
- Make the brochure as complete, honest, and upbeat as possible

- Trap yourself into needing completely new brochures each year because of dated information
- Be so specific that you disqualify too many interested people
- Let you lawyer write your brochure
- Make broad claims about unit sales, projected units, or quick returns
- Crow about "the opportunity of a lifetime" (the oldest cliche in franchising)
- Let the brochure become an "annual report" without a clear sales message
- Expect the brochure to do all of your sales work

A final point about the brochure also applies to the other promotional materials we have discussed in this chapter, and may be the most important thing to remember about all of your promotional efforts: Unless you have an extensive background in marketing and/or advertising, hire a professional (or professionals) to produce your materials. Truly effective copywriting, photography, and designing are difficult to do, and, like legal advice or financial assistance, are best left to experts. You should provide extensive input and retain final approval of all materials, but do not try to do everything yourself—especially things that professionals can clearly do better.

The franchise sales videotape

While we are on the subject of franchise marketing, we should mention that many franchisors are successfully using videotaped sales presentations as part of their lead follow-up program. Videotapes can often be produced for not much more than the cost of a good franchise brochure. And an effective videotape can tell your story in a way that even the best brochure cannot equal. It can bring your business "to life" with motion, music, and special visual effects. It can put the viewer face-to-face with the president of the franchise company and allow the prospective franchisee to hear and see the enthusiasm of people who constitute the market for your product or services—satisfied customers. It can demonstrate to a prospective franchisee what his or her role will be. If there is "romance" in your business, you won't find a better way to convey it than through videotape.

Traditionally, franchise sales videotapes have been used at trade and franchise opportunity shows to acquaint large numbers of people with a franchise program quickly. Many franchisors also use them as part of the sales process. But more and more franchisors—especially in the big-ticket range—are using the franchise sales videotape as a second lead follow-up tool. Some will mail it to the prospective franchisee with the brochure. Others make certain the prospect is fully qualified before sending a copy of the videotape.

With leads coming in and brochures (and even videotapes) going out, what comes next? In a word, selling.

Selling franchises

Some years back we met a former vice president of a major fast-food chain who had been responsibile for that company's fran-

chisee recruitment. We asked him, "How did you go about selling franchises for XYZ Company?" His answer was, "I sifted
through the applications the company received and eliminated
applicants who did not meet our standards." Of course, it is every franchisor's ambition to conduct a sales program in that manner, but until your company has 200 or 300 franchises, you will
be much better off taking a more aggressive attitude toward franchise sales.

Personnel

Remember, the selling of a franchise is a highly specialized skill,
and can't be done by just anyone. Whether or not you regard yourself as a salesperson, unless your company is large enough to
employ a franchise sales force, we feel very strongly that you,
as the franchisor, should sell the first few franchises yourself,
for the following reasons:

1. Nobody knows as much about the business as you do. You
   are the best-qualified person to explain the value and potential success of your business to potential franchisees. And it
   is important that your first franchisees see that the franchisor
   is personally involved in the business.

2. No one else will work as cheaply as you will. That may sound
   facetious, but we mean it. The early days of a franchise program is usually not the time to add as-yet-unnecessary personnel (such as salespeople) to the payroll. But more
   importantly, selling those early franchises should be the number one task on your agenda as a franchisor.

3. You should learn what selling your franchise entails so you
   have a full understanding of the process before engaging anyone else to master it. By doing so, you will also be in a position to train your first salespeople or sales brokers.

4. You will be in a position to have complete control over what
   is claimed about your franchise program and what is promised
   to prospective franchisees.

As your program grows, you may decide to establish an in-house sales staff or hire outside salespeople and/or business brokers. We generally recommend the former, because an in-house sales program usually costs less in the long run and is easier to control and direct than outside sales professionals or brokers. However, some companies lack the geographic representation to run a day-to-day sales program in all the regions in which they are selling franchises, and they turn to business brokers for assistance. Another advantage to using brokers is that they give you immediate use of experienced salespeople who are paid only if they sell franchises. A disadvantage is that you have little control over their day-to-day activities. Any company that uses business brokers should check with the broker's franchisor clients to determine how successful the broker has been in selling franchises. Frankly, most of our clients who have used business brokers for this purpose have reported unsatisfactory results.

We also recommend, as a precautionary measure, that you follow up each successful sales presentation, whether made by an in-house organization or an outside brokerage firm, by asking the franchisee to summarize his understanding of what you as a franchisor will provide. Some salespeople, in their eagerness to close the sale, make promises that you can't keep, such as offering to buy back the unit if the franchisee doesn't make money. Of course, for obvious reasons of accountability and ethics, the salesperson—when someone other than the franchisor—should never be in a position to ultimately decide whether a potential franchisee is accepted or rejected. That's your job.

The first call

Actual selling begins with the first phone call from you or your franchise salesperson to a prospective franchisee. The purpose of this call is two-fold: 1. To provide information and build enthusiasm about your program, and 2. Most importantly, to qualify the prospect. The actual qualification procedure—and it will continue throughout the sales process—is important not only as a means of screening prospects in order to select only those with a reasonable chance to succeed, but also to emphasize in the mind of the prospect that he or she must meet certain standards and criteria before a franchise will be awarded. These goals can be best achieved by a salesperson who exudes confidence in himself and his business. Whatever anxieties you may feel about selling your first franchises, you must not disclose them to the prospect. The fact is, you are not merely selling—you are also selecting.

In that regard, it is important to remember that it is never too late to disqualify a franchisee. If it is obvious from the first inquiry that a candidate could never hope to get financing, disqualify him. If, after being satisfied and impressed with a candidate every step of the way, you learn something extremely discrediting (of a criminal or ethical nature, for example) about him only days before the final papers are to be signed, disqualify him. Even if the candidate's lack of aptitude does not become evident until halfway through the training program, disqualify him. But to avoid these last two situations, it is far better that you learn every possible relevant factor—from money to character to ambitions and beyond—about your candidates before approving them as franchisees.

You can accomplish much of this during the first call by asking the right questions, then probing to be sure that the answers you receive are truthful. (Particularly in regard to their financial qualifications, you will find that prospective franchisees often tend to be overly optimistic.) To make the most of that first call, we recommend that you begin the qualification process by asking questions designed to provide you with information in three important areas: financial, readiness, and experience.

Financial. Don't be shy about asking whether the prospect is in a position to afford your franchise. "Mr. Jones, are you aware that the total investment required for this franchise is X dollars and that you will probably need a minimum in cash of Y dollars?" (Most franchisees put down between 20 and 30 percent and borrow the rest.) "Do you have either the borrowing capacity or net worth to be able to handle this kind of an investment?" These questions convey immediately that you are both selective and genuinely interested in the success of your franchisees. If it becomes clear that the prospect does not qualify on financial grounds, tell him so: "Mr. Jones, it doesn't sound like you have the financial capabilities to qualify as a franchisee at this time. However, should that situation change, we'd very much like to talk to you again."

Readiness. A prospective franchisee can be well-qualified from a financial standpoint, but not be fully prepared to move ahead. You should ask the prospect how soon he or she will be ready to seriously begin the process of becoming a franchisee. If the prospect will not be ready within a reasonable period of time (such as six months to a year), it's probably best to delay your meeting with him or her until then. Too much can change (for both parties) in that amount of time.

Experience. A recent survey of our franchisor clients revealed that—in general—their most successful franchisees have had some prior business experience. You may not want to make business experience a hard and fast criterion, but you certainly want to know who has had it and who hasn't. The degree of the prospect's experience might not be apparent in a brief list of his or her previous vocational activities. Specific questions should be asked, such as: "Have you ever held a sales position?" and "Have you ever managed people?"

Those who pass this preliminary test and who indicate an interest in your program should be invited to a meeting in your offices. Actually, this invitation can be considered a fourth qualifying procedure. We once encountered a franchisor who sent salespeople scurrying around the country to interview prospects, then wondered why his sales program was doing poorly. A prospect who refuses to come see you—even at the cost of a plane ticket—probably hasn't achieved a level of interest that will enable you to persuade him to commit his money and future to your program. You will do better to continue talking to such a person—

offering more information, telling him or her about the progress your franchise program is making—until such a time as he or she is willing to make that commitment. A person who has pre-qualified in these four areas becomes an excellent prospect indeed; such a person deserves your "best shot" at your face-to-face meeting.

By the way, if during this call (or subsequent phone calls) the prospect asks you to send copies of your franchise agreement and/or offering circular, politely refuse: "I'm sorry, Mr. Jones, but company policy prohibits me from sending our legal documents. I'll be happy to provide you with copies when you come to our office." The point to this is that you want to be available to answer questions about anything in the documents that the prospect may perceive as being negative.

The first meeting

At the meeting in your offices with the prospect (and, if desirable to both parties, the prospect's spouse), you will obtain additional qualification information. Have the candidate fill out a full application—including extensive business, financial, and reference information—and set up, for either that same day or very soon afterward, a schedule of full interviews between the candidate and the other principals in your program. At the first face-to-face meeting, also give the candidate the offering circular, explain its purpose and content—with special emphasis on points that you feel the candidate may regard as negative—and obtain a signed receipt. (Be sure that the receipts are kept in a safe place so that no one can claim that an offering circular was not provided on the day specified.) Also, stress that no money can change hands for 10 business days from the time the candidate receives this document.

This is the time to explain that the franchise agreement is fundamentally a non-negotiable document, that the franchise laws prescribe that, in effect, all franchisees must be treated equally— that each franchisee must pay the same franchise fee and royalty and that any material changes to the documents may, in some states, result in an expensive and time-consuming formal amendment process during which all franchise sales activity may be required to cease. (Some exceptions were covered in Chapter 7, but, at this stage of your program, the statement above should sufficiently cover any inquiries from prospects.) At this point, you should also ask for the name of the candidate's attorney, so that you or your attorney can explain the reasons for non-negotiability to him or her as well. We have found that most attorneys don't really understand franchise law; they must be told that they cannot regard a franchise agreement as they would a lease that they are expected by their client to make improvements upon.

The interview process

Either at the first or subsequent meetings, the candidate should be interviewed by a franchisee review committee made up of executives of your company. This committee should then confer about the acceptability of the candidate, and check the applicant's references and complete financial status and history. If the candidate is acceptable as a franchisee, notify him or her and set a date—keeping in mind the legal time limit following the issuance of the offering circular—for the closing of the sale. Have your attorney inform the franchisee's attorney of the date of the close.

The wait

Buyers often wonder during the 10-day waiting period whether or not they are making the proper decision. It is important that you talk to the buyer more than once during this period to answer any additional questions and to allay the normal fears anyone making a major decision will have. Buying a franchise is somewhat like buying a house, but the buyer doesn't have anything to look at or to show his friends and family other than a brochure and an offering circular. What negotiation is permitted under the franchise laws can be completed at this time. Specific delineation of the franchisee's territory, as well as other non-material matters can be agreed upon. During this period, it is important that you—and your staff—help keep the buyer happy, enthusiastic, and convinced that the correct decision has been made in the days before the closing of the sale.

The close

It is customary for the franchisee and his attorney and the franchisor and his attorney to meet for the closing. By this time, both attorneys should have come to an agreement on behalf of their clients regarding all negotiable matters. All that remains is for the agreement to be executed and for the initial franchise fee to be paid. This done, you shake hands. Congratulations, you have a franchisee. You are a franchisor.

And now comes the *real* beginning of your franchise program.

The Franchisee/Franchisor Relationship

If you have real ambitions to launch a successful franchise program, one of the first things you might do is to go out and have a plaque made. Hang it in your office to remind you: "The franchisee is king." Please don't read this as being too much of a tongue-in-cheek suggestion, because the hard, cold fact of the matter is that if the franchisees are not successful, the franchisor won't be either.

The franchisee/franchisor relationship, while a source of enormous potential success, also has a great deal of potential for conflict. As a franchisor, you need to provide the meaningful support and direction that will prevent major or minor catastrophes and help ensure the prosperity of your franchisees. History is replete with examples of dictatorial franchises that have failed or been rocked by franchisee revolts. In one such revolt, a group of Avis

Rent A Car franchisees sued their franchisor over alleged misappropriation of advertising funds. After Beatrice Foods, the parent company of Avis, was sold, the new buyer put Avis up for auction. Only after being offered a share of the company by the high bidder did the franchisees withdraw their suit.

As we stated in Chapter 1, Ray Kroc transformed franchising by regarding McDonald's franchisees as the literal life-blood of the chain. As Kroc realized—and as many successful franchisors have come to believe—a system's franchisees must be established and successful before the franchisor can ever hope to realize long-term success. However novel or sure-fire your business concept is, unless you provide your franchisees with adequate training and ongoing support, you may find yourself presiding over a failing business that is unable to live up to its potential.

Making the program work

Without disregarding what we have just stated in the previous two chapters, we believe that selling franchises is the easy part. Making them work is the hard part. And you can't make them work at all unless you have selected the right kind of franchisees and then given them the appropriate training, support, and supervision.

In the period immediately following the sale and extending through the first few weeks of opening the new franchised unit, the franchisor should be accessible to assist the franchisee in site selection, lease negotiations, equipment purchases, selecting initial inventory, and grand-opening promotions. The last few days and hours before the franchisee opens his new store are emotionally (and often, physically) trying, with the franchisee knowing he has his life savings on the line, wondering whether customers will materialize, and if they do, whether he'll be able to handle them. But the franchisor—in the person of a franchising agent, executive, or (mainly in the early days of the program) the franchisor himself—should be right there, reassuring and providing last-minute instructions. For the first weeks or months afterward, all the franchisee should have to do is pick up the phone and call for answers to questions, until the business seems so simple that these earlier worries are forgotten. By this time, the hand-holding that the franchisor has been providing no longer is needed—the "children" have grown up.

However, as the franchisees become more knowledgeable in the operation of the business, and about their customers, they can no longer be treated like fledglings. The franchisor becomes more of a consultant, or a senior partner. The franchisor should have a planned program of support, including store visits by the field supervisor (who, at least initially—as we have said—may be the franchisor). Accompanying each royalty check should be reports on sales, and when the field supervisor visits the franchisee, these reports should be reviewed, along with the costs of goods and labor, and any other issues that may need attention.

Typically, in an established franchise, a field supervisor oversees 10 to 25 stores and should know what every operating unit in the territory is doing in terms of sales volume, inventory, payroll, and so forth, and should be aware of the competitive environment around each of those units. This is the kind of information the supervisor then relays to the franchisor in regular reports. The field supervisor should be available to assist the franchisee, as needed, with supplier relations, employee relations, community relations, and financial matters, acting as a liaison between the franchisee and the franchisor's headquarters to notify the franchisor when the franchisee needs additional support or training.

Providing support

While these reporting routines and structures are necessary for a successful franchise program, they can be meaningless unless they are backed with a very real and substantial commitment to franchisee support. As in any successful relationship, communication is the key. Open lines of communication—literally as well as figuratively—can help both parties keep abreast of each other's situations. Keeping track of the facts and figures about your franchisees is, of course, important, but there are factors to keep in mind that can affect sales figures and other numbers; location, regional economy, advertising support, and competition are just some of the most obvious and critical ones. A franchisor that can—individually or collectively—understand and appreciate any given franchisee's complete situation is better positioned to maintain a healthy relationship with that franchisee.

When Ray Kroc personally visited McDonald's first franchises, he often spent a few minutes picking up trash in the outlet's parking lot before he met with the franchisee. This not only underscored the importance Kroc put on cleanliness, but it also showed the franchisee and the outlet's employees that the franchisor cared about them and their needs. While you may not go as far as Kroc did, a combination of two-way communication, an understanding of the franchisee's situation, and firm but reasonable direction can help keep your franchisees successful—and keep your entire franchise program healthy.

The special needs of conversion franchisees

In general, conversion franchisees need less support of the start-up or "hand-holding" variety, and more firm direction than the average business-format franchisee. Because these franchisees already have experience in the franchisor's line of business, major re-education may be necessary. Their preconceived ideas on how their business should be run may be totally contrary to the way the franchisor wants the business run. A Mr. Build franchisee quoted in a 1984 *Inc.* magazine article admitted that the two hardest parts about becoming a conversion franchisee were replacing the name of his business and relearning how to run his business after years of habit and independence.

One company that has successfully minimized the support it must provide its conversion franchisees is Re/Max, a real estate company that has sold 1,000 units in less than 10 years and expects to have 1,500 outlets in 1987. Unlike traditional real estate offices which require a salesperson to split commissions with a broker, Re/Max allows the salesperson to keep all commissions but pay a monthly share of the office expenses and a fixed fee to the broker, who is the franchisee. The franchisee makes a profit and attracts salespeople with proven sales ability who are able to pay the monthly brokerage fee. The parent company is able to use its resources to provide computer services and a referral network instead of training programs.

Franchisee associations and councils

Many successful franchise companies form franchisee associations and/or regional or national franchisee councils. The best time to organize such a group is right in the beginning—not when there are problems and the franchisees are threatening to revolt. A good example of an effective franchisee group is the International Pizza Hut Franchise Holders Association (IPHFHA), which was formed in the early stages of Pizza Hut franchising to provide a communications link between the company and its franchisees. The IPHFHA monitors marketing and promotion plans and has an equal say with the company about new products and advertising campaigns. Two IPHFHA members and two franchisor representatives serve on a committee that gives final approval to the chain's multi-million-dollar advertising budget. Membership in the IPHFHA is mandatory for franchisees, with dues being two percent of sales per store, per year—yielding a huge advertising budget and making the group independent of the franchisor. With its economic clout, the IPHFHA has also been able to enjoy collective buying advantages, and even formed its own insurance agency, which resulted in a savings of 30 percent off regular insurance rates for its members.

Initially, local or regional franchisee organizations can be formed. In their early stages, these associations serve as a forum for the franchisor to provide group instruction or disseminate information which is important for all franchisees. However, as the franchise program grows, the association should be turned over completely to the franchisees. The association should also be encouraged to meet on a regular basis, to elect officers, and to provide a forum for franchisees to openly discuss ideas. These associations can coalesce a group of independent businessmen into a unified force and can be a very effective tool in developing a successful franchise program. The franchisor should remain available to the association to make announcements, give special presentations and awards, and generally provide guidance.

The next logical step is the formation of a national franchisee council, with representatives from each local or regional group. A by-product of forming a national franchisee council is often the formation of an advertising advisory council, which reviews advertising agencies suggested by the franchisor and provides direction in the development of advertising campaigns. This process allows the franchisees to participate in the advertising program, defusing some of the criticism that results when a program isn't as effective as franchisees perceive it should have been.

It is important that these councils understand that their role is advisory, not adversarial, to the franchisor. Many franchisee organizations have become quite powerful, and they've been successful in obtaining special federal and state legislative protection, as well as instigating class-action lawsuits. Importantly, while franchisee organizations can inspire or instigate lawsuits against franchisors, they cannot sue under their own name because they usually are not the parties harmed. Nor can they collectively bargain for better franchise agreements, since the courts have found that to constitute a horizontal restraint of trade. A number of states, however, have protected the right of franchisees to form such associations and have passed laws specifically forbidding a franchisor from restricting the franchisees' right to do so.

New ideas from franchisees

Whether collectively or individually, franchisees are an important source of new ideas, as well as an impetus to the entire program to adopt changes that are good for the business and help keep it competitive. McDonald's credits its franchisees for coming up with the idea of opening the stores for breakfast, which now accounts for 15 percent of its system-wide sales, as well as with developing some of the chain's most famous and popular products, notably the Egg McMuffin, McD.L.T., Filet-O-Fish, and Big Mac.

We previously mentioned Dahlberg Inc. (which makes and sells hearing aids), and how the company converted its dealers into franchisees. In an interview with *Inc.* magazine, president Jeff Dahlberg noted the front-line savvy of franchisees, and said, "We're under the gun to give our franchisees state-of-the-art products. They're very aware of their competition and what they need to beat them." Another Dahlberg corporate officer agreed, adding, "They'll ask much more of a company than a bunch of dealers. If you invested your money and made a commitment to one company, you'd expect a lot, too. We never had that here before. I'd say the change has made Dahlberg a much better company."

Although the very nature of franchising is the successful replication of a tried-and-tested concept, this certainly doesn't mean standing on a pat hand. The implementation of successful new ideas is important to the continued prosperity of a franchise program. We feel there are few people in a franchise program more qualified to develop new ideas than individual franchisees. Most franchisees know their local market—and its needs and wants—much better than their franchisors do. Every-day exposure to customers and their needs can help a franchisee realize what product and/or service modifications or changes are best suited for a particular region, market, or even time of day.

Franchisees should strive to properly serve their customers—just as franchisors should strive to properly assist and nurture their franchisees. While it is inexact to say that franchisees are to franchisors as customers are to franchisees—the relationship is more complex than that—it is not far-fetched to suggest that a franchisor's primary goal should be to fully serve and support his franchisees. As Ray Kroc and many others have discovered, this can be an important step on the road to the success of a franchise program.

Financing Your Franchise Program

Writer Somerset Maugham sagely observed, "Money is like a sixth sense—you can't make use of the other five without it." Nor can you launch and support a franchise program without money. However, the question is not simply whether or not your company has the money for expansion, but whether or not you have the ability to raise additional capital when you need it.

Of course, it helps if you have some liquidity. While taking the Franchisability Test in Chapter 4, you may have been interested to see that one of the questions focused on how much capital you could devote to a franchise program. The ratings may have surprised you, however, when you found that having $100,000 was only good for 4 points out of a possible 10.

Franchising can be a lucrative business, but, as the saying goes, it takes money to make money. Few companies can afford to embark on a franchise program without some source of financing, whether it's through a bank loan, a private stock offering, or a venture capital arrangement of some sort. And yet, experience has shown that despite the impressive track record of franchising, the financial community appears to be no more eager to assist successful businesses in becoming franchisors than any business seeking money for expansion purposes—and perhaps less so than if the non-franchise expansion consists of brick and mortar. Part of the problem lies with banks, investment brokerages, and other financial institutions who have barely a rudimentary understanding of franchising and its income-producing potential. But it is also true that business owners who become franchisors are often more sales- and marketing-oriented rather than finance-oriented. This chapter may be helpful to both groups, but is particularly designed to explain to franchisors—in layman's terms—their financing options.

How much do I need?

Franchises are developed in phases, and various types of financing may be needed at some, or all, of them. To begin with, financing may be needed to develop the prototype unit on which the franchise program is based. Franchising, of course, is a method of expanding a proven concept. To create a business and achieve the kind of success that is prerequisite for franchising, many entrepreneurs obtain some kind of financing in the form of personal loans, either from friends or relatives, or from banks. However, today more and more people are using an easier route to obtaining capital to start—or perfect—a business. Having built equity in their homes, they are refinancing and putting the equity to work.

The second stage of development where capital—and, therefore, financing—usually is necessary is in the development of the franchise program itself. The cost of putting together all of the elements we have outlined in the previous chapters and of supporting the program in its early stages—a period of approximately 12 months—might be as low as $50,000 or as high as $150,000—or more, depending upon the complexity of the program. Of course, not all of this money will be paid out at once. But you will be spending a sizeable percentage of it in the first year. On the other hand, before the year is out you may well be deriving income from franchise sales.

Two principal questions related to franchising confront the new franchisor: "How much money will I need?" and "Where will I get it?" As a first step to answering the question of need, you must answer two others: "How much cash do I have that can be spared for this program?" and "What can I use for collateral should I decide to seek financing?" If you have decided that $150,000 will carry you through your franchise program to the point where franchises can be sold and income generated, and if you have $40,000 in cash and at least $110,000 in collaterable property or merchandise, then you have answered the question of need and can proceed to the question, "How do I get it?"

But a simple definition of need in these terms is not always possible, especially for a franchisor. Every franchise is fundamentally service-oriented, and unless your business involves substantial real estate ownership or deals in high-ticket merchandise it may not have enough collateral to offer a bank in return for the money you require. If you tend to be overly optimistic, you may inaccurately assess the time required to achieve profitability, a common failing, especially among businesses with short track records. If your business is five or 10 years old, you've probably experienced some ups and downs and will be able to factor both into your projections. If your business is relatively new and you've experienced nothing but success, your tendency may be to assume the success can be transferred to your franchise program in much the same time-frame. The key word in correctly assessing financial need is "time." You can hope for overnight success, you can know in your heart that your projections are conservative, but you must allow for the possibility that your goal will simply take longer than you imagined it would. Of course, if you do that you may make another mistake. You may borrow too much. But in our opinion, that is better by far than borrowing too little.

If you do underestimate the amount of time it takes to reach the X-factor mentioned in Chapter 8, you will run out of money before achieving the goals you've set. Should that happen, you may be required to change your program, your ability to borrow can be seriously affected, or, in severe cases, your business can be lost. The moral is: Before you borrow, do everything within your power to accurately assess your needs based upon a hard, unemotional look at the factors governing your business and its future and based upon the opinions of experts you trust.

How do I get it?

Assuming, however, you have taken a liberal view of expenses and a conservative view of income and assuming that your final figure remains at $150,000, you are ready to answer the question: "How do I get it?" If you can provide cash or collateral for the entire amount, of course, the problem is relatively easy to solve. Most banks will be happy to give you money that they feel they can recover at any time at a favorable (to them) rate of interest. But let's make the problem more complicated. Assume that you have only $80,000 in collaterable property and merchandise, which means that you are hoping to obtain $70,000 of the $150,000 total without hard assets to pledge in exchange if you are unable to repay the loan.

Commercial banks

Are banks suitable targets for such loans, or would you be wasting your time? Typically, it is true, banks want heavy collateral before they make a business loan, and unless your company is adequately capitalized, either through your own cash reserves, existing cash flow from the business, or other private sources, it will be difficult to obtain bank financing for the frontier costs of a franchise program. When banks look at your balance sheet and at the valuation of your company, they tend to discount the principal asset of your business, which is the knowledge, experience and ability of you and your employees.

Despite this tendency among banks as a whole, some banks are, nonetheless, becoming aware of the franchise phenomenon. For example, 10 banks in the United Kingdom and five banks in Canada have formed programs for financing franchises. One of these, the Royal Bank of Canada, has provided more than $400 million to franchisees and franchisors. In the United States, Atlanta's Citizens and Southern National Bank has recently established a division for financing franchised businesses, and we predict that more U.S. banks will follow suit, especially after national banking laws are passed, probably in the 1990s.

Even banks without formal franchise finance programs may be approachable by businesses seeking franchise financing. Although banks are always asset-based lenders, because of deregulation, competition, or other factors, some are more aggressive than others and will lend on a combination of credit worthiness, cash flow, and collateral. Of course, in such cases even the most liberal bank will file a personal property lien on all of your assets as head of your company.

If you are seeking a bank loan and your current bank lacks aggressiveness, you may want to go shopping for a bank that does. When you've found the type of bank you're looking for, you need to "cultivate" your banker. First, you must convince him or her that the market for your goods or services is growing, not declining. To do that you really should back up your claims with market data and solid business forecasting. You may even help your cause by adding to your banker's knowledge of franchising (perhaps by giving him a copy of this book!). But bankers base decisions partly on intuition. You must come across to them as knowledgeable, responsible, and personable. You can have the world's best business plan, but if the banker doesn't like you, look elsewhere. Your present bank may fit this profile, but if you're not positive, don't take it for granted. Conditions change and banks change. Last year's bull can be this year's bear.

Incidentally, wherever you go for money, the more sophisticated the presentation of your concept, the better. A clearly-written business plan incorporating detailed, comprehensive projections is well worth the time and money involved in its preparation. One of the most straightforward practical guides to developing a business plan is presented in Joseph A. Mancuso's excellent book, *How to Write a Winning Business Plan*. We highly recommend a review of that text.

SBA loans

All your best efforts with your bank may nonetheless go for naught. In that case, you have the option of applying for a Small Business Administration (SBA) loan, either through your commercial bank or directly to the SBA. The SBA will guarantee as much as 90 percent of the loan, up to a maximum of $500,000, greatly reducing the risk for the commercial bank. The SBA also offers long-term loans for five, seven, 10, or even 12 years, whereas the terms of most commercial banks are considerably shorter. In addition, the loan-to-collateral ratio for an SBA loan may be smaller than the ratio for a bank loan, perhaps four-to-one or five-to-one, as compared to one-to-one or two-to-one. The SBA generally requires home equity and/or business assets as collateral, and as Jerry Gardner of the SBA explains, the applicant must demonstrate his commitment to the business: "We want someone to put it all on the line and pledge everything." For the SBA to make a direct loan, the applicant must have been rejected by two banks, yet nonetheless be considered a good risk. The SBA will provide you with a list of approved lenders (there are about 1,000) as well as booklets that explain the constraints placed on these loans, such as what the money can (and cannot) be used for, how much can be applied to inventory, how much to real estate, and so on.

Applying for an SBA loan can be cumbersome because of the paperwork involved, but *getting* the loan may be much easier. *Entrepreneur* magazine found that 93 percent of the qualified people who apply, and who fully and properly complete the application, are approved. Even more surprising, considering the fact that the SBA is a government agency, is the *Entrepreneur* finding that the average application is cleared within three weeks. Even so, only three percent of the people who open new businesses each year apply for SBA loans. (In fiscal 1986, the SBA guaranteed more than $133 million worth of loans to franchised businesses.)

Equity financing

A bank or an SBA loan is essentially a kind of debt financing; you borrow money that you are expected to repay with interest. Another alternative to consider after you have evaluated your monetary needs is equity financing. In this case you are not seeking a lender, you are seeking an investor—someone who will provide you with capital in exchange for the rights to some of the future earnings of your company.

In our experience, most business owners prefer to look for asset-based over equity financing when launching a franchise program, although too often their reasons are emotional: "I'm not selling any of my business to anyone!" In fact, the goal of most successful business owners is sooner or later to seek equity financing through a private or public offering. Quite bluntly, that is often how businesses reach their ultimate potential in size and revenue and how their owners become rich. (Notable exceptions are a few businesses that have managed to grow while remaining wholly owned by families.) The question for most companies regarding equity financing is not "Whether?" but "When?" And frankly, it is probably a mistake if you are just developing your franchise program to think about seeking equity financing. If you give up 25 percent of your business too early in the game, the amount of money you get for that 25 percent will be modest. Then you may be tempted to sell another 19 percent to get more. If you're not careful, before long you will lose control of your company. It's far better as a rule to bite the bullet in the early (prototype) stages of a business venture by tapping friends and relatives, later going to asset-based lenders when you decide to franchise for additional growth capital, and finally, when your concept is proven and in a strong growth mode, looking for equity financing.

Nevertheless, for one reason or another, equity financing may be your best—or only—option if your dream of becoming a franchisor is to be realized. One way of utilizing the technique of equity financing while minimizing its long-term effects upon ownership of your company is by seeking funds through a Small Business Investment Corporation.

SBICs are venture capital groups licensed by the SBA to provide capital for small businesses in return for equity in those businesses. (A list of the approximately 1,000 SBICs in the United States is available from the SBA.) SBICs are structured in such a way that for every dollar the SBIC partners put into the fund, the SBA allows them to borrow up to $4. In other words, if a group of investors puts up $5 million in cash to form an SBIC, the SBA will allow them to borrow an additional $20 million, giving them a $25 million pool from which to make loans to small businesses. Normally, a business that seeks a loan from an SBIC agrees to put up shares in the company as collateral for the loan and further agrees to buy back those shares at some later date, at an agreed-upon price, with a stated rate of return. Of course, SBICs fund relatively small amounts of equity; in fact, the average SBIC investment in 1985 was only $192,000.

The most common form of equity financing of course is through the issuing of stock. Initial public offerings (IPOs) are generally made by companies seeking $2 million or more and we will discuss them in more detail later in this chapter. You can, however, issue stock without going public. For example, you can make private placement offerings directly to investors through investment banking firms, selling stock in your company to a previously defined and restricted number of buyers, and with certain dollar limits on the amount of stock sold. Should you decide to investigate this method, a securities attorney can assist you in complying with the federal laws regulating such issues, specifically regulation D 17 C.F.R. 230.504-506.

As your program grows

As we have suggested, most franchisors are better advised to wait until their franchise program has been successfully implemented before seeking equity financing. At this point, when you have anywhere from 20 to 100 units in operation, your business plan may call for an amount between $2 million and $20 million dollars or more to establish additional company-owned-and-operated units in key markets, not only for the purpose of generating additional franchise sales, but to use as flagships for training management and supervisory-level people. At this time your company will show a far higher value than it did before you franchised. Past franchise fees and royalties, as well as income from the sale or lease of products, services, and real estate to your franchisees, can be used to project future earnings. Now, to obtain the funds you need to accelerate your franchise development program, you may decide to pursue equity financing, either through venture capital sources, or an IPO.

Venture capital sources

More than 600 venture capital firms in the United States provide private investment capital to companies that are unable to obtain debt capital from traditional or conventional sources or equity capital for their shareholders. Often, venture capital firms examine hundreds of potential investments before making even one deal.

As a rule, a venture capital group will prepare a valuation of the company and forecast its earnings over a five-to-seven-year period. The group also may prepare detailed financial projections that will include an analysis of capital requirements for the next three to five years, the timing of the input of those funds, what the debt will be, the rate of return, and the internal rate of return for the venture capital group. This analysis is submitted to the entrepreneur, and if the two parties come to an agreement, the capital is provided in exchange for a note and an option to participate in the ownership of the company. The venture capitalists secure their investment by taking stock in the company, the amount depending on the level of risk, although it is also possible that part of the loan will be asset-based and referred to a third-party lender. Again, the danger to the borrower in not meeting the projections is that the venture capital firm can step in and take control of the company through its ownership of stock and the entrepreneur can end up losing the company.

If the proper venture capital firm is selected, it can be a valuable partner because it can not only help with debt, by matching part of its investment with borrowed capital from an affiliated bank, but it can also provide assistance and advice. The firm can help in hiring qualified management, obtaining financing for franchisees, providing advice in mergers and acquisitions, in accounting and tax treatment, and even in attracting high-quality franchisees. To more fully appreciate what venture capitalists are looking for in analyzing any investment, we would suggest reading *Investing In Private Companies* by Arthur Lipper III.

Some franchise companies combine venture capital investments with an initial public offering of stock. In the first private placement offering, the venture capitalist gets warrants or options to purchase additional stock when the company goes public, at ar agreed-upon price that is lower than the market price on the date of the IPO. By the time the second round of stock is offered, the company's value, and thus the stock's value, should have increased. This strategy, from the venture capitalist's viewpoint, can be effective for getting money out of the company and putting other investors' money into it. To accomplish this usually requires the assistance of an investment banking firm and an auditing firm, since the company will need certified audited statements going back three years. Of course, you may be fortunate and find an "angel"—a wealthy individual or small group of individuals—who will provide capital without the formal application needed for a public offering.

IPOs

The first thing you should understand about an Initial Public Offering is that instead of using it to raise several-hundred-thousand dollars, you will spend at least that much and probably more in legal and accounting fees and expenses for printing and distributing the offering circular to launch your IPO. That's the bad news. The good news is that the $2 million dollars or more raised by the offering (and there is not much point—considering the time and effort involved—in seeking less than that) will cover those expenses and then some.

The second thing you should know is how your business will be valued and what the consequences will be. "Going public" is, as we have indicated, simply a means of selling part of your company to a large group of investors for the cash you need to enable it to reach its full potential. To accomplish this, you will need to persuade an underwriter (either a brokerage house or an investment banking firm) that your company has sufficient current strength and good prospects to justify an IPO. The underwriter's job is to determine the value of your company and then to sell whatever amount of stock you decide to issue to its investor customers.

One of the keys to having a successful offering is to choose the right underwriter, a company with a good reputation and a large number of monied investors. But choosing an underwriter is only part of the battle. Your goal in an offering is to have your company valued as high as possible and to sell as small a percentage of it as necessary to obtain the funds you need. The underwriter's goal is to please its investors by selling them stock that will quickly appreciate in value. The simplest way for the underwriter to achieve this goal is to place an unrealistically low value on your company, so that the stock's price rises immediately after issuance. One way to avoid undervaluation is to become thoroughly versed in the methods used by underwriters to value companies and to rigorously apply them to your own situation. Another is to find an experienced financial consultant who understands underwriting techniques and who will negotiate on your behalf.

Following is a list of some of the major publicly-owned franchisors and publicly-owned companies with franchise holdings.

Adia Services, Inc.
Alexander & Alexander, Inc.
Allied Capital Corporation
Benihana National Corporation
Brock Hotel Corporation
Business Cards Tomorrow, Inc.
Captain Crab
Casey's General Store
Chi-Chi's, Inc.
Chock Full O'Nuts Corporation
Church's Fried Chicken, Inc.
The Coca-Cola Company
Control Data Corporation
Convenient Food Mart, Inc.
Cucos, Inc.
Cutco Industries
Dairy Mart Convenience Stores, Inc.
Dahlberg, Inc.
The Deltona Corporation
Dunkin' Donuts, Inc.
Entré Computer Centers, Inc.
The Firestone Tire & Rubber Company
Fuddruckers Franchising, Inc.
General Motors Corporation
The B.F. Goodrich Company
The Goodyear Tire & Rubber Company
Hilton Hotels Corporation
Holiday Corporation
Inacomp Computer Centers, Inc.
Jamco, Inc.
Jerrico, Inc. (Long John Silver's Seafood Shoppes)
Manpower, Inc.
Marriott Corporation
McDonald's Corporation
Medicine Shoppe International, Inc.
MicroAge Computer Stores, Inc.

MPSI Systems, Inc.
Munford, Inc. (Majik Market)
NuVision, Inc.
The Olsten Corporation
Pay-Fone Systems, Inc.
PepsiCo, Inc. (Kentucky Fried Chicken, Pizza Hut, Taco Bell)
The Pillsbury Company (Burger King, Häagen Dazs)
Postal Instant Press
Pizzeria Uno
Pizza Inn, Inc.
Playboy Enterprises, Inc.
Ramada Inns, Inc.
Rax Restaurants, Inc.
Ryan Homes, Inc.
Sbarro, Inc.
Shoney's, Inc. (Captain D's)
Sizzler Restaurants International, Inc.
Skipper's, Inc.
Snelling and Snelling, Inc.
Staff Builders, Inc.
Swensen's Ice Cream Company
Taco Villa, Inc.
Tandy Corporation (Radio Shack)
Topsy's Shoppes, Inc.
TCBY Enterprises, Inc.
TW Services, Inc. (Hardee's Food Systems, Inc.)
Twistee Treat Corporation
Uniforce Temporary Personnel, Inc.
USA Cafes (Bonanza)
Vie de France
VICORP Restaurants, Inc.
Wendy's International, Inc.
Western Steer—Mom 'n' Pop's, Inc.

Financing for franchisees

Franchisors are not alone in needing capital. People often need money to buy franchises and for the real estate, equipment, and working capital they need to operate them. Later, franchisees need capital to establish additional units. Some businesses need capital to provide financing for their customers, especially when high-ticket products are being sold. To obtain capital, franchisees can use some of the same options as franchisors have—refinancing personal holdings, applying for conventional bank loans, and applying for an SBA loan. To qualify for an SBA loan a franchisee must be the sole owner and operator of the business, employ fewer than 500 people, and have a sound business plan. Being a member of a minority can also help.

(We should point out, however, that prior to 1985, 85 percent of all franchisors surveyed by the International Franchise Association would not permit their franchisees to obtain SBA financing. Until then, an SBA rule required as a condition of franchise loan approval that franchisors agree to defer collection of royalties while franchisees were in default of SBA loan obligations. Yet even after the SBA made royalty deferral a "consideration" rather than mandatory, SBA offices continued to impose royalty deferment as a "condition" to loan approval rather than merely as a "consideration.")

Some finance companies work with franchisees as well. Franchise Capital Corporation has an unusual limited-partnership approach. It buys the land and building for multi-unit restaurant and fast-food franchises then leases the property back for a term of 20 years with an early purchase option. Another company, Franchise Finance Corporation, raised more than $800 million between 1980 and 1986 for the sole purpose of financing real estate for franchisees of a major hotel/motel, fast-food, and truck stop franchise. Westinghouse Credit Corporation pursues franchisee financing when the franchisor meets the following conditions: 1. Has a proven concept; 2. Owns three or more units; and 3. Has been in business for three years or longer. Bank of

America Credit Corporation and General Electric Credit also provide financing to franchisees.

Of course, franchisors who assist franchisees in obtaining financing also further their own interests. TCBY, a chain of frozen yogurt stores, established a financial subsidiary as part of its IPO for the purpose of buying and leasing restaurant equipment to its franchisees, achieving the following four goals in the process:

1. Helping to facilitate the sale of franchises;
2. Establishing a separate profit center;
3. Enabling them to promptly identify franchisees in trouble, determine how seriously, and to provide help;
4. Putting them in a better position than any other financial institution to dispose of the equipment in the event of a default.

Some franchisors provide financing for franchisees by deferring franchise fees or other start-up costs. However, such practices can be a trap; franchisees who are too thinly capitalized can do more to harm a franchise program than help it. A franchisee with a significant amount of money on the line is not only in a better position to reduce the debt service, but more committed to making the franchise unit profitable.

Usually, franchisees make less use of venture capitalists as a source of financing than franchisors, primarily because the amounts involved tend to be lower and not worth giving up part of the business to obtain. However, area franchisees sometimes find it desirable to sell equity in their businesses in order to raise funds for developing a territory rapidly before the competition arrives. Allied Capital has financed a number of such franchisees both with direct loans and through its venture capital funds.

In summary, financing for franchisors (and to a lesser degree for franchisees) is becoming more available from a variety of sources. The key to finding the best source of financing at the price you are willing to pay is to shop for it.

The Future of Franchising

Imagine: The year is 2030. A great cheer goes up as the space shuttle lands at the colony on Mars. As the passengers disembark and walk through the spaceport, they are greeted by the sight of the familiar Golden Arches adorning the recently opened 25,000th McDonald's. "Over 1 Trillion Sold," reads the sign...

Science fiction? Perhaps, but who knows where the aggressive expansion of franchising will next lead. What *is* most nearly certain is that whatever the future of retailing and business holds, franchising will play an important part in it. The U.S. Department of Commerce calls franchising "the wave of the future" and predicts that by the year 2000 franchise sales will total half of all retail sales. In 1985, franchise sales represented 20 percent of the gross national product, up from 10 percent *just two years earlier.* For more than 20 years, sales from franchise outlets have grown at an average of 10 percent annually. The Commerce Department predicts total sales in excess of $870 billion by 1990. The watchwords in retailing, and therefore in franchising, are convenience, specialization, and segmentation, and franchises that can continue to successfully combine any or all of those qualities will do well in the future.

"Megatrends" in franchising

In 1986, John Naisbitt, head of the Naisbitt Group and author of the best-seller, *Megatrends*, compiled a study on the future of franchising for the International Franchise Association, and among the trends identified are the continued decline in product and trade name franchising, and the growth of business-format and conversion franchising. Total business-format franchising has been the fastest growing form of franchising since 1972, and Naisbitt predicts that it will continue to be so, projecting a growth rate of 11.5 percent for the five years following the report. As we discussed in earlier chapters, this type of franchising is particularly applicable to service businesses, as the U.S. economy has shifted from the production of goods to the provision of services, beginning in the years immediately following World War II. Also, business-format franchising is appealing to people who want to own businesses of their own but want to minimize the risk involved. Persons new to the business arena are drawn by the simplicity of this concept, which also attracts people with some business experience who seek a proven program that requires less of an investment than starting an independent business. The study also sees continued growth in conversion franchising, as entrepreneurs develop strategies for unifying and marketing fragmented industries.

Naisbitt identified the top 10 franchise industries for the period 1985-1990, and summarized their growth on the following table:

ESTIMATED GROWTH OF TOP FORMAT FRANCHISE INDUSTRIES, 1985-1990

Business	Sales (in billions)		Annual % Growth
	1985	1990	
Restaurants (all types)	$ 48.9	$ 86.1	12.0
Retailing (non-food)	18.8	33.6	12.3
Hotels, motels, campgrounds	14.6	22.5	9.0
Convenience stores	12.3	19.4	9.5
Business aids and services	12.1	21.3	12.0
Automotive products and services	10.6	15.9	8.5
Retailing (food other than convenience stores)	10.4	15.9	7.0
Rental services (auto, truck)	5.3	8.9	11.0
Construction and home services	3.7	9.2	20.0
Recreation, travel, entertainment	1.8	6.6	29.0
Total top ten	**$138.5**	**$238.1**	**11.5**

These rankings reveal some interesting facts. For years now, industry experts have been predicting a slump in the fast-food industry, saying that fast-food franchises have saturated the market. However, Ray Kroc appears to have been right when he said, "Saturation is for sponges." A healthy 12 percent growth rate is predicted for fast food and more franchisors are entering the field almost daily. In 1986 a *Venture* magazine list of the 100 fastest-growing franchises included 23 fast-food restaurant chains. As for McDonald's, various business analysts have long been predicting the company would peak, but in 1985 its growth continued at the rate of one new restaurant every 12 hours.

The appeal of specialization

We have seen an increase in specialization in retailing recently. In the food-service industry this has led to more demand for ethnic foods and health foods, and has created franchising opportunities for such narrow product lines as frozen yogurt, chocolate-chip cookies, and gourmet ice cream, to name a few. This specialization has also affected non-food retailing, particularly in appealing to the more affluent consumer, with more boutique-type franchises, such as the Aca Joe and Benetton clothing stores. These franchises also reflect the segmentation of the market, with these boutiques (for the most part) aiming for the upscale segment. Even in the automotive market, we've seen specialization to the *nth* degree, with franchises that provide detailing for luxury cars, and, at the other end of the spectrum, lube and filter jobs for domestic cars at $9.95.

The trend to build more economy-priced hotels and motels also reflects the trends toward specialization and segmentation. Family travel is becoming increasingly common, making economy units more in demand, as well as easier to construct and operate. As consumers look for the most value for their dollar, they turn to the familiar names of the larger hotel chains, with their toll-free phone numbers and standardized units, which means that the ability of independent operators to compete is decreased. Here, conversion franchising plays an important role in bringing together smaller motels in order to achieve a marketing identity. The business traveler and the affluent pleasure traveler are still factors to consider, however, and hotels are developing marketing programs that recognize the need to be different (or at least appear different), touting such programs as business "club" hotels and all-suite accommodations.

Convenience stores, rather than wanting to be different, appear to want to become all things to all people. Instead of carrying just the basic necessities—milk, eggs, cigarettes, and soda pop—now the stores offer gasoline, video rentals, dry cleaning services, catering, automatic teller machines, and prepared foods of all sorts. Initially, the convenience stores expanded their services in response to competition from grocery stores, which had extended their hours. Now, some convenience stores are partially invading the instant food-service realm of fast-food restaurants. And, in fact, some convenience stores are incorporating other franchises within their units, e.g., 7-Eleven with Church's Fried Chicken.

Another fast-growing area of franchising is in business aids and services, which range from employment agencies to copying services. The growth of these businesses coincides with the country's shift toward being an information society, and with the advances in new technology. This new technology has created a demand for workers with special skills, especially for short-term projects, and hence, the need for temporary-help agencies and specialized temporary-help agencies, such as AccounTemps and TRC. Changing technology has also created office equipment that may only be needed on occasion (such as color copiers, facsimile machines, or special computer accessories), opening the door for franchises that can offer that service.

The automotive aftermarket is another strong area for franchises, especially since the number of full-service gas stations has declined, and people have begun keeping their cars longer. While some car owners prefer to do repair work themselves, most look for assistance. Franchises, with their name recognition and standard of quality, are in a good position to capture these customers. By offering quick oil and filter changes or lube jobs, they also deliver something else—convenience, one of the primary benefits of franchising.

Convenience in the marketplace

To consumers, convenience has always been one of the hallmarks of franchising. From roadside restaurants to corner stores of all types, convenience has been and will continue to be a strong attraction of franchises. Today, convenience means more than location and hours open. The convenience of service has become a focal point in the construction, home improvement, and cleaning services category, and these services are likely to continue to grow in popularity.

The Naisbitt study found that consumers are willing to pay for convenience and quality, which will benefit home-service franchises and construction franchises. Consumers will pay for a name they recognize, which may continue to drive many small operators out of business or convince them to join a conversion franchise, such as Mr. Build.

If consumers are willing to pay for convenience, they seem doubly willing to pay for recreation and leisure-time activities. Recreation, travel, and entertainment franchises made up the fastest-growing area surveyed in the Naisbitt study, with annual revenue growth averaging 30 percent since 1980. Travel agencies, movie theaters, video rentals, and miniature golf courses are among the successful franchises in this category. The country's general interest in health and fitness has had an effect on franchising as well, with a number of franchises that offer diet counseling, exercise training, home health care, and medical care. Home health care is the fastest-growing segment of the health care industry, with growth spurred by insurance companies' refusal to pay for lengthy hospital stays, and a growing older population. Several franchises have entered the market, often competing directly against hospitals which offer some form of home health care. A subsidiary of H & R Block, Inc. owns the 210-unit Medical Personnel Pool franchise and projects that the franchise will double in the next two years. Three other franchises, Harmony Health, Health Force, and Nursefinders, see an equally bright future, particularly as the government's cost-containment policies escalate the need to care for patients in their homes, often at 10 to 20 percent of the cost of a hospital stay.

Franchising's future challenges

Ironically, one of franchising's chief advantages also is one of its biggest problems, and will continue to be so. The fact that it is relatively easy to start a franchise—and even easier to *buy* one—will attract under-capitalized and unprepared franchisors and franchisees. There still will be examples of unscrupulous franchisors and unsophisticated franchisees, despite years of legislative and regulatory efforts to eliminate them. Franchisors and franchisees will expect to be protected, as much as possible, from failure, and this probably will lead to more litigation and more legislation. Franchisors will want to maintain strict control over their systems, and may be reluctant to share the decision-making responsibilities with their franchisees. However, franchisors who do not allow some level of genuine participation and input from their franchisees may be in for a bloodbath, as franchisees sue— particularly in cases where franchise agreements are not renewed, royalties are raised, or marketing strategies fail. To avert this, we believe that savvy franchisors should treat their franchisees as partners and continue to support franchisee associations and involve them in corporate long-term planning. Those who do not may face ruinous court battles as franchisees collectively show their strength.

Another irony of franchising is that while it will be successful in creating more jobs, there may be no one to fill these jobs. As we've said, the American economy is rapidly changing from being product-oriented to service-oriented, and the Naisbitt study predicts that by 1995 some 73 percent of the work force will be in service-industry jobs. Many of these jobs will be low-paying and offer little in the way of advancement—the kinds of jobs traditionally done by teenagers. Yet, already fast-food restaurants are claiming that they can't interest teenagers in filling these positions, even at salaries above minimum wage.

The trend toward specialization in retailing will add another complication because sales clerks will be required to be much more knowledgeable about their products. Franchisors will be faced with the task of designing programs and operating schedules that are attractive not only to the franchisee and to the consumer, but also to the work force. Franchisors and franchisees will have to look to other segments of the population for employees—including housewives who may have little or no experience, handicapped individuals, and senior citizens. In 1986, McDonald's launched its McMasters program to train employees 55 years of age and older. In a May 1987 *Chicago Sun-Times* article, Anne Le Fave (who, at 83, was McDonald's oldest employee at that time) told how much she enjoyed working at McDonald's, and said that businesses need to realize that "older people are the best workers...I feel great. I am not going to sit home and wait for my Social Security check and get feeble."

Franchisors may also have to begin offering incentives other than pay, including scholarships for teenage workers, day care facilities for working mothers, and improved health benefits and more frequent rest breaks for older workers. As the elder population continues to grow, franchisors should look for new ways to meet their needs, which may mean changes in the way existing businesses operate, as well as the creation of entirely new franchises.

Women and minorities increasingly are turning to franchising as a way to enter the business world, and smart franchisors have been only too happy to accommodate them. Burger King, Pizza Hut, Taco Bell, Kentucky Fried Chicken, and Baskin-Robbins all have minority recruitment programs for franchisees, offering special financing options and other incentives. It's good public relations and reflects a level of social responsibility, but it's also good business, since these minority franchisees can help capitalize on inner-city markets. Other franchise programs have been very successful in recruiting women. The Diet Center claims that 98 percent of its franchisees or subfranchisees are women. Women At Large, an exercise franchise aimed at larger women, has sold nearly all of its franchises to women. The Bureau of Labor Statistics discovered that in the period 1974 to 1984 the rate of increase in the number of self-employed women was 74 percent, three times greater than for men. As women rise through the ranks in traditional businesses, they will gain the experience and the capital to enter franchising in ever larger numbers.

As competition increases, franchisors will look for new markets, and that search will lead many franchisors to foreign shores. According to 1984 figures compiled by the U.S. Department of Commerce, 328 companies were franchising internationally—with a combined total of more than 27,000 outlets. Furthermore, one in 13 of these franchisors reported earning more than 10 percent of their total income from foreign outlets. We feel that American products and business practices, especially franchising, will be accepted in other countries. Japan, in particular, is proving to be a fertile ground for the sale of U.S. franchises. The franchisor who designs a franchise program that is consistent with the cultural demands and economic conditions of a foreign country, and then works within the existing business structure of that country, has a high probability of success.

Eight trends for the future of franchising

In conclusion, we see eight major trends emerging in franchising in the coming years:

1. Record numbers of companies will franchise their businesses...For the reasons mentioned throughout this book.

2. Corporate restructuring and the need to earn a higher return on assets and equity will bring about a wave of acquisitions of company-owned chains and subsequent re-sale to franchisees. Once the chains are acquired, the individual operating stores will be sold to franchisees at a higher price than the original buy-out, generating instant profit, establishing ongoing income through royalties, and resulting in hands-on, caring unit management.

3. Franchisors and franchisees will expand into each other's— and outside—businesses. Franchisors will diversify by owning franchises (becoming franchisees themselves), by buying other franchisors, or by developing new franchises. Franchisees will diversify by becoming franchisors of new concepts or by becoming franchisees of more than one business.

4. More institutional money will be attracted to franchising companies. As outlined in Chapter 11, institutional investors—in the form of potential stockholders or investment corporations—are, in general, pumping large amounts of money into various franchise ventures. There are currently more than 70 franchisors (or parent companies of franchisors) who offer public stock, and this number should continue to rise.

5. Conversion franchising will grow in dramatic proportions. Conversion continues to be the answer in fragmented industries that lack an identity—and, importantly, a clear market leader—and need a unified approach to give the concept an edge in the marketplace. In addition, more and more franchisors will offer low-cost conversion options to existing businesses simply for the purpose of growing more quickly.

6. More franchisors will be acquired by large companies. By acquiring proven franchisors, corporations will seek to reap the benefits of franchising while avoiding many of the pitfalls of entering an unfamiliar market cold. However, this method is not foolproof—costly mistakes can occur due to lack of proper vision, a misunderstanding of a new field, or the replacement of entrepreneurial spirit with corporate bureaucracy.

7. Combination franchising will flourish. If one franchise is good, two or more can be better. That unspoken philosophy led to the growth of "franchise rows" in towns and cities across the country, but more recently it has given rise to a new form of franchise symbiosis. Wendy's and Baskin-Robbins, Taco John's and Bresler's 33 Flavors are just two examples of franchisees sharing the same facilities while continuing to operate independently of one another. We believe that cooperative ventures of this kind will continue because experiments show that start-up costs can be lower for both parties and sales can be higher. In the cases mentioned above, the ice cream franchise has increased traffic in off hours for the restaurants and the restaurants have provided higher traffic for the ice cream shops at regular meal times.

8. Franchising will make the world smaller. The "one world" that populist politician and author Wendell Willkie predicted in his book of the same name remains remote, but franchising will take us another step in that direction. The global distribution of products and, to a lesser degree, services is already taking place. Franchising, by fostering the international cross-pollination of business concepts, will make cultural differences less and less distinct. U.S. franchisors are leading the way, but in the next decade we predict that scores of franchisors from many countries will become household words around the world.

Franchising today may be a long way from establishing the first interplanetary McDonald's (or Holiday Inn or H & R Block or Century 21), but it has also progressed significantly from its beginnings in trademark and product licensing to its "rebirth" through business-format franchising to its present level of acceptance and all-pervasiveness. The important thing to remember is that franchising has as much to offer today—and tomorrow and beyond—as it did in its early days. In fact, if anything it has more to offer now. It is a business system that is "user-friendly" to bright and committed businesspeople and entrepreneurs, whatever their backgrounds or concepts, however large or small their companies. Increasingly, the question is not: "Should we franchise?" The question is: "How can franchising in one or more of its many forms help us to achieve our expansion goals?" When a company approaches franchising in that manner, a new and exciting world of opportunity can open up.

Franchising has grown to become one of the most identifiable and publicized forms of business extant. It is the American dream with a safety net. It is Ray Kroc and Tom Monaghan, Burger King and Midas mufflers; it is a multi-billion-dollar industry with roots on nearly every big-city street corner or small-town Main Street. It is a remarkably efficient distribution vehicle that many business owners have ridden to riches—and *you* could be next. That, truly, is the franchise advantage.

Index